MATZOHBALL

MATZOHBALL

by

SOL WEINSTEIN

Combustoica
a prose project of About Comics - Camarillo, California

MATZOHBALL
by Sol Weinstein

This novel originally appeared in abridged form in the December, 1965 issue of *Playboy*. This edition reprints the 1966 expanded novel, with new revisions made 2011 by the author.

Published by Combustoica, a prose project of About Comics.
WWW.COMBUSTOICA.COM

Rights inquiries? *rights@AboutComics.com*

Table of Contents

DEDICATIONS

(This includes the half of the U.S. population not cited in the
dedications to *Loxfinger**)

CELIA LEVINE
In Memory

DON AND SANDY BARNETT

JUDGE PHILLIP FORMAN

SAM AND ANN RABINOWITZ & FAMILY

PAUL GRAY
the "International Humorist'
and
MARK RUSSELL
the "Washington Wit"
who are sorely needed as regulars on the TV "talk" shows

ISRAEL (COKE) RUBIN

MICKEY DANER
...had he not loved honor more,
he would have loved it less

RON & CAROL AXE DR. RALPH ROBBINS
... "dream doctor," healer of the sick,
the Sandy Koufax of Miami Beach

SANDY KOUFAX
on general principles

DR. DAVID J. SILVERSTEIN
Of Lancaster, Pa., who has taught his Pennsylvania Dutch clientele to
know vot good is

RON & JEAN FRIEDMAN

---

* Pocket Books, Inc., 1965, $1.

BELOVED UNCLE H. J. SHERMAN
Of Sherm's Deli, Long Branch, N. J.

BELOVED TANTEH RIVA ROSENBERG
JACK AND DORIS SHERMAN, JACK AND MARY SHERMAN,
JACK AND FRANCES ROSENBERG, JACK AND SOPHIE
ROSENBERG, JOSH SHERMAN, SHULAMITH AND LEO
RUTKOFF & FAMILY, MR. AND MRS. DICK AXE, GAIL COATES,
JACK CURTIS OF THE LATIN CASINO, LOU AND RUTH DELIN,
JOHN DELBRIDGE, DR. KEN HENRY, AARON LENOFF, STAN
AND MINDY LEDERMAN, GIDEON AND ELISHEVA GLAZ, BOB
LANE, JAY LAWRENCE, DICK MATHEWS, BOB NESOFF, DON
PALMER, MIKE ROSENFELD, DR. JOHN E. TURNER, ALICE
HELGESON

ABEL GREEN
to whom Variety is the spice of life (and the bread)

EARL WILSON
and his B.W., B.M.L., T.W.A., R.C.A., M.I.T., etc.

SGT. MICKEY BRANNON, JERRY GAGHAN, "RED"
BENSON, LEON BROWN, FRANK BROOKHOUSER, SANDY
OPPENHEIMER, EMIL SLABODA, BIFF HOFFMAN, HERB RAU,
LARRY KING, PHYLLIS BATTELLE, JANET CHUSMIR, MIKE
McGRADY, THOMAS W. LIPPMAN, YUDEL SUSSMAN, CHARLIE
SCOTT, DON SCOTT, FLORENCE (CHOO-CHOO) BLOCK

SYLVIA AND LIPPY EISNER, SCOTT SHUKAT, JANET AND
BETTY EISNER, BERNIE SOHN, HARVEY AND HARRIETT
BLATT, ALLAN DELIN, BENNIE AND JENNIE LINDENBAUM,
SANDRA AND ARNIE SIMON, MILTON LEVINE, BOBBY AND
MONA COURTNEY, CAROLE AND ARNIE BERNSTEIN, DORA
KAPLAN, EDDIE AND ALICE GREENBERG, RONNIE AND
STEVIE GREENBERG, LOUIE AND YETTA CRAVITZ, ROSIE,
RICHARD, AND ELYSE RUDOW, SAM AND CEIL CRAVITT,
HANNAH AND LENNIE ROTNOFSKY, SAUL AND HELEN
ROTNOFSKY, LENNIE AND RUTH MARKOFF, TANTEH EVA
LINDENBAUM, SIDNEY AND CHARLOTTE LINDENBAUM,
YOUIE AND CHARLOTTE CAPILUPI, MARVIN AND NORMA
GATES, PHYLLIS FISHMAN, CY AND MALVINA VOGEL,
MARVIN AND MARSHA ROSENBERG, BOB AND JANE AMOROS,

FREDDIE AND JOSIE TRAUM, HERB AND RAE STEIN, MEYER AND BESSIE GRUSMARK, ISADORE AND JENNIE KRAKOWER, RABBI AND MRS. WILLIAM FIERVERKER, SID AND RUTH SHUCKER, LEO AND FLORENCE FEINMAN, GENE AND JOYCE KONDASH, MOLLY LEVINE, LENA LEVITSKY, SYLVIA WEINSTOCK, MARTY AND MIRIAM LAIBOW, WALT LAMOND, MARV AND ERICA LAZOFF, MORRIS AND ADRIANNE BERENBAUM, FRED AND NETTIE BERK, GEORGE COHEN, MAX YOUNG, RUTH GOVER, RON AND JUDITH EDELMAN, OWEN LASTER, DENNIS PAGET, ESTELLE RAE ADLER, "DOC" GREENE, MARK BELTAIRE, SHIRLEY EDER, ED FISHER, BOB GOLDMAN, NORMIE LAYTON, MAX ASNAS, BILL GAINES, AL FELDSTEIN, NICK MEGLIN, JERRY DE FUCCIO, JOHN PUTNAM, LENNIE BRENNER, the "boys" from MAD MAGAZINE.

MICKEY MANTLE
Who hits 'em 500 feet

JOE E. LEWIS
Who hasn't walked, that far in thirty years

And...
NANCY BROWN
Of Plainfield, N. J.

"Remember, Mr. Bond, a house divided is a split level."

—M.

1
The House of Good Taste

"Plain or egg matzoh?" asked the gash of a mouth under the thick, neatly trimmed Mandarin moustache.

There was no answer from the bearded patriarch three feet away whose soft brown eyes were riveted to the blue-black metal object in the right hand of the questioner.

"Again, my dear, dear Rabbi, I shall put the question to you. Plain or egg? And remember... a single ill-advised motion on your part, and one squeeze of this"—the Walther PPK Reuther automatic in the corded right hand dipped in a mocking bow—"will transport you instantly to some far-distant Talmudic academy where your sainted predecessors, Rabbis Hillel and Akiba, are doubtlessly waiting to engage you in some wearisome polemic regarding a fine point of Mosaic law."

Again there was no response from the stoop-shouldered clergyman (possibly he was too engrossed in parsing the sentence), but the slightest of tics in the right eyelid did not escape the cold, proficient, Volga-blue ones of the gun wielder, Colonel Sergei Svetlova, owner of the professionally bored voice. Inwardly the stocky Russian seethed with exultation, an emotion betrayed by the pale pinkish tongue which licked at the wet woundlike gash of a mouth. For the colonel was on the verge of pulling off a stunning counterespionage thrust for the KGB, intelligence apparatus of the Soviet Union.

"For shame, Rabbi," the colonel bantered. "Surely you are a poor representative of Israel's famed hospitality. A Soviet official interrupts his important routine to pay a courtesy call upon your nation's esteemed housing exhibit and there is no solicitous hand to proffer a cup of tea, a mouth-watering Israeli sweetmeat. Ah well, no matter," the colonel sighed with resignation. "The scion of a Don Cossack learns early in his life to be resourceful. I shall take my own repast, dear Rabbi. Now, what would you suggest? The roof? Possibly a shutter? Or the door, that portal to Jewish learning and understanding? Yes, the door."

Colonel Svetlova's left hand touched the door lovingly, then dug the nail of the index finger into its silvery exterior and, with a quick deft slash, peeled away a gleaming six-inch whorl. The finger jabbed at the interior. There was a loud snap. With a gouging lunge, the entire left hand came away from the door with a jagged section of white-and-brown-flecked board; bore it to that gash of a mouth. There was a crunch as the teeth of Colonel Svetlova closed upon it; the voice emitted a grunt of satisfaction.

"Plain, I should say, from my limited knowledge of the Judaic tradition. Is it all plain or is there perhaps some *egg* matzoh in the other sections of this wondrously constructed, prefabricated ranchhouse of yours? Come, come, dear Rabbi. It is fruitless to delay or prevaricate further. The evidence in my hand and mouth should clearly indicate to you that Operation Matzohball is blown. Not only is it blown, but I have bagged, certainly, the world's most famous ghost in the bargain!"

2
Rotten Roger: The First Call

It had been a humdrum day for Colonel Svetlova (a pen name derived from his family's inordinate fondness for perspiration) in his top-floor office in the dull brown three-story edifice on Ulitza Ouspenskaya, the building talked about only in furtive whispers by the average Russian in the street. With good reason: it is the headquarters of the dreaded KGB.

He had leafed through the overseas cables, sorting through the usual run-of-the-mill stuff filtering in from all over the globe. New York: "We have sketchy reports of a new American missile, the IRTBM, which is designed to carry a 10-megaton payload to Moscow, after preliminary stops at 14th Street, Penn Station and Times Square." Jakarta: "The Chinese have bested us in an important psychological battle to ingratiate ourselves with Sukarno. Their gift subscription of *Playboy* arrived before ours." (That damned slow-witted Major E. B. Yevomat! He would have to pull the major out of his cushy Indonesian assignment. But there was still a chance to recoup. If prima ballerina Tamara Villbebetta would make a hasty trip to the dictator's private quarters and let him paw *de deux....)*

Then the call had come... four sentences delivered in a matter-of-fact voice, suggesting that the caller thought as little of betraying his country as he would dispensing weather information.

Shocked, Colonel Svetlova had stood mute for a moment, then allowed an unthinking "My God!" to escape from his trembling gash. And a tactful, "Who does not exist, of course," in the event his secretary, Sergeant Toma Treshkova, might note in her daily report that he had let slip a decadent religious expletive.

An old hand at KGB politics, Svetlova was positive Sergeant Treshkova had been planted in his office by his superior in the section, General Gregori Bolshyeeyit, who would stop at nothing, he knew, to discredit him.

"Sergeant Treshkova," he said with ill-concealed annoyance. "Let us hear the playback of that telephone call."

The sullen face said, *"Da,"* and Sergeant Treshkova, with some effort, extricated her lumpy body from her straight-backed chair and waddled across the room. Svetlova noted with amused disdain her oaken calves encased in the new patterned stockings favored by Western women, and recently introduced into Moscow society. They represented her lone desultory bid for femininity, he realized, but merely transformed those legs into two disgusting rolls of varicosed chickenwire. Her feral odor, that of a newborn sloth, made his nose twitch; he was further revolted by her toadlike expression, the generously pocked complexion, her damp weedy strings of lusterless blonde hair, the pendulous sacklike breasts reminding him of a wheat shipment from Canada, the warts on her nose, eyelids and gums.

As she pushed a doughy finger against the playback button on the huge tape recorder which occupied an entire wall, she whistled through her harelip a snatch of a tune she had been enamored with of late, a melody of American origin entitled "I Feel Pretty."

There was the pht-pht-pht of scraping tape, then an almost inaudible beep, which brought a wry smile to the Svetlova gash. It meant, naturally, that his telephone was bugged, the listener quite obviously General Bolshyeeyit. Svetlova knew this to be so from his conversations with Corporal Anna Annatevkah, the general's long-legged, dark-eyed secretary and Svetlova's own plant. With Anna's connivance he had managed to place a miniaturized camera in the flower bowl on Bolshyeeyit's desk. In the colonel's secret file were dozens of close-ups of azalea petals, whose value Svetlova could not as yet ascertain. But he threw nothing away.

He forgot all about his internecine warfare with the general when the voice on the tape broke in.

"Colonel Svetlova, this is Rotten Roger Colfax with information of the most vital import concerning a plot, instigated against the Soviet Union by the State of Israel, known by the code name

'Operation Matzohball.' The model house assembled by Israel for display at the Moscow International Home Show in the Institute of Architecture is made entirely of matzoh—its exterior cloaked by a capitalistic substance known as Reynolds Wrap so that you will be led to believe it is aluminum siding. It is the plan of M 33 and 1/3 to dismantle the house at the conclusion of the show this evening and disseminate pieces of the matzoh to key leaders of Jewish communities throughout the Soviet Union, each particle stamped with the Hebrew words, 'Take Heart; You Are Not Forgotten'; thus reviving the kinship between the Zionist nation and its brethren here and breeding further discontent with life under your rule. In addition, the man posing as the spiritual advisor of the Israeli delegation at the Home Show is no rabbi but, in fact—"

"Colonel Svetlova. A word, please."

The last words of the sentence were smothered by the deep bass of a lean hawk-faced man in the uniform of a general who had poked his head into Svetlova's office: General Bolshyeeyit, commander of the Internal Affairs Section of the External Affairs Division of KGB.

"*Da,* Comrade General!" barked Svetlova, leaping to attention. His stiffened hand smashed the portion of skull above his right eye in a smart punishing salute. Pain flooded his face; an angry red flush crept over the bulletlike bald head. He staggered for a second; clutched his desk to steady his swaying body.

General Bolshyeeyit refrained from permitting a grin to purse his thin ascetic lips. The general knew quite well that there was a steel plate in Colonel Svetlova's head, the result of a terrible wound suffered on a dangerous mission behind the German lines in World War Two, when a tiny vial of nitroglycerine secreted in the sexual organs of a female Gestapo agent had gone off during an exhaustive search by the colonel. He also knew that his deliberately frequent appearances (with the concomitant necessity for saluting) would someday cause the colonel to drive the plate into a highly vulnerable portion of his brain, destroying himself on the spot. A confidential surgeon's report on Colonel Svetlova's monthly head X rays had apprised him that precisely one hundred more of those enthusiastic salutes would achieve the desired result.

"Colonel, how do you plan to counterattack 'Operation Matzohball,' as our colleagues in the Israeli secret service have picaresquely named this amusing little venture?"

Svetlova's mouth dropped open. "How did—?"

"I know all things, colonel," the general cut in brusquely. "That is why I occupy the office I do."

"Comrade General," Colonel Svetlova began, "I should enjoy the privilege of smashing this Zionist plot myself. After all, the telephone call from this Rotten Roger Colfax, obviously a pseudonym used by a traitor in Israel's M 33 and 1/3, came directly to me. The caller knew the correct telephone exchange, which is highly classified, proving he, indeed, has access to material of the most delicate sort. He, no doubt, is aware of my special background in Jewish matters."

"Granted," said General Bolshyeeyit, dragging on an expensive Mother-of-Pearlman cigarette holder. Svetlova noticed with surprise—and satisfaction—that there was no cigarette in it. Excellent, he thought. This superior of mine is not infallible at all. I shall yet hold his job someday.

The general inhaled again. "You have my leave to crush this Zionist conspiracy. But take heed. If your informant, this Rotten Roger Colfax, is correct, the so-called rabbi may be an exceedingly difficult man to deal with. Have you men you can trust?"

"To be sure," said Svetlova. "I have sent for two very tough, capable men, Nikolai Federenko and Alexei Norelco. They will accompany me and stand watch outside the Institute."

General Bolshyeeyit's brow wrinkled. "Federenko I know of. An absolute brute and well-fitted for this kind of work. I, however, am not acquainted with Norelco. You can vouch for him, I trust?"

"*Da,* General. I have known him since he was a little shaver. Stupid, but massively constructed and doglike in devotion. He would lay down his life for me."

"I hope that will not be necessary," said the general. "Well, *chorosho!* In that case I shall wish you a speedy conclusion to this absurdly pathetic Israeli affair. *Dobri noch** Colonel."

"I shall not fail you or KGB, Comrade General," the Svetlova gash twisted in sheer fervor. And, as though a Jack-in-the-box touched by a spring, he leaped to his feet and once again brought that rigid hand to his brow in a rapier slash of a salute, exploding a white-hot ball of agony in his skull. He moaned aloud.

Again General Bolshyeeyit managed a straight face. That one must have taken a terrible toll of Svetlova's tortured tissue, he

---

*   Good night.

reckoned. "Ninety-nine, Colonel Svetlova," he said softly, and, returning the salute, strode off in his usual measured step.

"Ninety-nine?" Svetlova was puzzled. "Ninety-nine? Now what in the name of Father Lenin did that ice-blooded martinet mean by that?"

Slowly, gingerly, he let his fingertips steal across his churning, pain-smitten head. It must be ignored, he told himself; time to work. "Sergeant Treshkova!"

She reappeared at the door. "Bring me the dossier of this *Ivriski Shpion**" he snapped, scribbling a name on a pad and handing it to her.

A deep hearty laugh made him look up. "Imagine, dear Colonel. I have forgotten my gloves, ha! ha!" It was General Bolshyeeyit whose white suede gloves were quite safe in the deep pockets of his trenchcoat.

"I shall find them at once, Comrade General," said Svetlova, who, of course, could not, despite several frantic seconds of overturning pillows, peering under chairs, shuffling papers.

"Ah, well, the GUM department store, I am sure, has another pair in stock. Again, *dobri noch*, Colonel." The general's hand flicked a casual salute, compelling Svetlova to return it. This time the jolt of pain sent him reeling into the wall. General Bolshyeeyit, preferring not to notice his fellow officer's suffering, offhandedly remarked, "Ninety-eight," and left the room.

To Svetlova it seemed his skull was crisscrossed with a network of barbed wire. To steady himself, he lit a Kemal, a superior Turkish cigarette which combined the finest, most aromatic tobacco leaf with a blend of the choicest halva. Inhaling and letting the tranquilizing smoke invade his lungs, he forced himself to pore over the folderful of material pertaining to the Hebrew agent in question.

With an American-made Bic pen, which operated somewhat haphazardly on paper, but was excellent for writing on ice, he underlined a Hebrew word, "mezuzah," a word which meant the tiny cylindrical symbol of the ancient faith worn about the neck by all observant Jews. It contained a portion of the sacred scrolls.

But not this man's mezuzah!

"This religious artifact," he read from the dossier, "has been transmuted into a murderous device. By pressing the Star of David on its front it releases a sharp needle upon whose tip may be found an instantaneously acting nerve poison called

---

* Hebrew spy.

SOL WEINSTEIN

Molochamovis-B. The Hebrew word Molochamovis is Biblical in origin. Let the agents of our service beware. It means 'The Angel of Death!' "

As though he were in mortal peril that very moment, he reached into a drawer, pulled out the Walther PPK Reuther, shoved a clip into it and placed it in his shoulder holster. He remembered something else. From another folder, this one containing various miscellaneous materials dealing with Jewish history, customs, peculiarities, he removed the present year's Jewish calendar. He looked at his Russian calendar; matched it against the corresponding date on the Jewish one.

"Ah... ha!" he said. "According to this, the Passover holiday is a week away. Rotten Roger's data seems to fit in perfectly. It certainly would take a few days for couriers in Moscow's Jewish community to ferry the matzoh to their coreligionists in other cities. And the International Home Show does conclude this evening. What an innocent, natural thing for the Israelis to do, dismantle their sample house quite legitimately; then make arrangements for transporting it to the airport by truck. Of course, there would be a terrible misfortune between the Institute and the airport. An accident, perhaps. Or a theft. And, alas, the prefabricated house would disappear. I cannot let such a thing come to pass."

He ruminated upon the eye-opening telephone call from Rotten Roger. An unbelievable pseudonym! What was the man's purpose? Money? He had no doubts that Israel's secret service, working on the most insignificant of budgets, was underpaid. Yet, he had never before come across a case of defection concerning M 33 and 1/3 personnel. A grudge, perhaps? Failure to be promoted? Then a negative thought occurred to him. Could this "traitor" be sending KGB up a blind alley to obfuscate some even more devious Israeli plot?

Colonel Svetlova had been compelled to revise his opinion of Jewish determination and fortitude after reading the dossier of the Israeli operative whose snapshot lay in his hand. It had been taken by a seemingly harmless vendor of Italian ices near the famed Fountain of Levi, a bustling landmark in Rome's Jewish quarter, where, legend had it, good fortune would come to him who tossed three Cohens into the azure waters. A series of regrettable drownings had made the *carabinieri* crack down on the traditional practice. The vendor, one Ronzoni Sonoboni, a paid KGB agent who took these pictures as a matter of routine, had snapped it with a tiny camera secreted in his lemon-ice scoop. The face was dark, cruelly handsome; the eyes cold and gray; a sensual mouth set in a hard line of decision; the total effect: the countenance of a man deep in the throes of some murderous thought.

This man, Svetlova reminded himself, is bad business. He holds an Oy Oy number in M 33 and 1/3, which grants him a license to kill! I must exercise ultra caution. To still his nerves, he pulled the cork from a bottle of kvass, kvenched his thirst kvickly and pressed the buzzer.

"Send in Federenko and Norelco immediately."

They entered, both clad in shabby black suits, with bellbottom trousers, covered by dirty trenchcoats. Federenko was first: a tall, swaggering, strong-arm man of about forty-five, an expert in karate, judo, aikido and ring-a-levio; then Norelco: short, squat, with enormously muscled arms which when applied in a bear hug could splinter an opponent's vertebrae. The little man paused to gaze longingly into the face of Sergeant Treshkova who had ushered them in. "You... hee hee... very beautiful woman." A simpering blush stole across his vacuous peasant face. She also reddened and, flashing a warm inviting glance back at him, left the room whistling. "I want that woman, Comrade Colonel. I not see beautiful woman such like she back on farm."

"And you shall have her, if all goes well tonight, my dear Norelco," Svetlova assured him. "I am told she is very exciting in the bedchamber, my friend. Now," and the levity left his tone, "we visit our Middle East neighbor's extraordinary dream house."

Athrob with tension, Svetlova's chunky legs pistoned him into the darkened street. Thump! He collided with a figure in the shadows. His hand flew to his holster; the gun was out completely when a familiar chuckle aborted his action.

"Would you slay your superior, whose only crime is a relaxing stroll on this bracing April night, my dear Colonel Svetlova?"

"Forgive me, Comrade General. For a moment I thought—"

"But there is no time for thought, Colonel. You have a hard day's night ahead of you. I shall not detain you further. Again, *dobri noch.*" The hawk-face crinkled its friendliest smile and the general saluted.

So did Svetlova.

General Bolshyeeyit, knowing his face was hidden by shadows, did not suppress his grin this time as he watched Federenko and Norelco prop up Svetlova, whose knees had buckled, and drag him into the car.

Blowing a smoke ring, he said tonelessly: "Ninety-seven."

3
Marriage of Steel

This was the prelude to the drama now being enacted in the cavernous Institute of Architecture, whose sole occupants were the bald Russian officer and the stoop-shouldered holy man upon whom he trained his automatic.

An excellently crafted disguise, Colonel Svetlova conceded. The face composed of sunken, desiccated flesh, muddy-brown eyes (contact lenses, of course); a typical rabbi's shiny, dark-blue gabardine suit exuding odors of tobacco, schnapps, and herring; payis—the curly forelocks of the Orthodox Jewish set, the Mea Shearim, dangling disconsolately; faded white talis (the prayer shawl) with Mogen David wine-purple striping draped about the bent neck; the full-blown, unkempt black-tinged-with-grey beard; and the literally crowning touch: the yarmulkeh, a black skullcap.

Prior to entering the side door to the Institute used primarily by the departed janitorial staff, Colonel Svetlova had seen the sample homes trucked away by workmen of the countries involved. Next to last to go had been Nigeria's, which had featured its new mud-brick hut designed by the famed American builder of mass housing developments, William J. Levitt. The soon-to-be Nigerian Levittown would see thousands of low-cost huts springing up under the equatorial sun. It would engender a vastly different way of life for the Nigerians who would become typical suburbanites, commuting to Lagos, the capital city, on the 6:15 water buffalo, bitching about gardens invaded by "that goddam swordgrass," lazing on their patios at sundown, watching the hyenas drag off the Avon lady.

When only the State of Israel's gleaming ranchhouse remained, Svetlova had stationed his thugs at the loading platform and startled the rabbi with his drawn weapon. Then he leveled his accusations.

The rabbi's eyes blinked in agitation. "Sir, I am at a loss to explain the unique composition of this house. And this curious reference of yours to the 'world's most famous ghost'... what do these bizarre things mean? I am but a humble servant of the Lord, mine and yours, though your society has chosen to reject Him."

"Ah," the colonel said wearily. "I had expected more intelligence from you, Rabbi. Or should I say more accurately— Oy Oy Seven? To utilize a poor pun from your own holy works, why beat about the burning bush? The game is up. A compatriot of yours, in fact, a member of your espionage branch, has told all. Or does the name Rotten Roger Colfax mean nothing to you?"

A tremorous hand stroked the beard in wonderment. "I have truly never heard of that name, sir." Then the hand began to stray slowly downward, still stroking the beard, sliding toward the neck.

"Stop!" the colonel snarled. "Touch that mezuzah and I shall present you with a third eye. I'll relieve you of that, *Rabbi*," the appellation spat with hatred. Svetlova's left hand shot out, ripped the chain brutally from the old man's neck and hurled it upon the asphalt-tiled floor. His right jackboot stomped upon it again and again, the impact splitting asunder the cylindrical symbol of the rabbi's faith.

"Blasphemy! Blasphemy!" screamed the old man. "To crush the sacred scrolls as though they were a cigarette! What do you hope to accomplish by this inhuman outburst?" The gnarled hands vibrated in righteous anger.

"Just removing the viper's sting, dear Rabbi," and the colonel bent down and felt among the pitiful wreckage for the needle. There was none. He unrolled a mashed scrap of paper in his free hand. There were Hebrew letters imprinted upon it.

And it was the colonel's turn to wear a puzzled look. "But... but..."

"I shall demand an immediate apology from your government, sir. This barbarous conduct against a man of God...."

"Silence, man of God! You are now in the enlightened milieu of Soviet socialism. We need no hoary legends to sustain us. But," and his voice took on its coloration of cunning again, "let us see if you are truly what you claim to be. We shall commence by—" the left hand sprang out—"by tearing off this handsome, albeit false, beard."

From deep down came a volcanic, tormented roar. "*Gottenu!* spare me from further indignity. Better let me die now." Tears glistened in the eyes. Svetlova, rattled, uncertain, tugged at it again; then the forelocks, the hair.

"They are... real." The gash of a mouth had lost its hauteur. It now twitched with indecision. "And the eyes... filled with tears. Real tears. How could contact lenses produce such a phenomenon?"

The rabbi, heartened by Svetlova's rapid loss of composure, had regained his own. "Why are you doing this to me, sir?"

Svetlova looked down at his boots. "My dear Rabbi. My dear, dear Rabbi." There was genuine penitence in his speech now. "It appears that I have made an unforgivable mistake. You are, after all, a guest in the Soviet Union, Rabbi, uh... Rabbi..."

"Rabbi Chair. Spiritual head of Congregation Bethel Leslie, 354 Georgie Jessel Boulevard in the port city of Haifa. Graduate of the Moses Maimonides School of Rabbinical Training and Fund Raising, 1924. Author of several well-known treatises on Jewish lore and law; among them: 'The Stage Delicatessen—A Look at the New Judaism,' 'The Negev Desert: World's Most Frightening Sand Trap,' coauthored with an American named Arnold Palmer, and my latest study, 'Should Religion Be Allowed to Intrude at a Jewish Wedding?'"

"Impressive credentials, indeed," muttered Svetlova, who jotted down the data in a black leather notebook as the rabbi intoned them. "Your first name, please, Rabbi Chair."

"Morris."

"Of course." He closed the notebook. "Now, I do not think there is anything to be gained by your lodging a formal protest about my admittedly..." he sought to inject the proper adjective... "uh... untoward methods of interrogation. I apologize for them personally. The fact remains," and he reverted to his officiousness again, "that innocent dupe though you may be you are nonetheless guilty indirectly of complicity in this shameful plot to foment unrest among our... uh... respected—and quite happy—Soviet citizens of Jewish lineage."

Rabbi Chair's mien was thoughtful. "My dear sir. I, of course, had no knowledge of this 'plot,' as you term it, but I am bound to tell you that morally I must align myself with its aims: If one of them is to make the Passover matzoh available to Russian Jews, I am in full sympathy with it. This stratagem would have been quite unnecessary in the first place if your State Baking Trust was not deliberately ignoring the need for matzoh during the coming holiday period. In general, Russian Jews would not be so restive if they were permitted to carry out a full-fledged program of Jewish activities, both religious and secular... if your book publishing agencies would print all the prayer books required by a Jewish population of three and a half million, instead of the pitiful few they do... if your building inspectors would cease their deliberate policy of condemning Jewish synagogues on trumped-up pretexts and then never reopening them nor permitting new ones to be constructed... if Jewish criminals mentioned in your newspapers were simply termed criminals, minus the sly references to their religion, a technique which cannot help but restoke the ancient coals of anti-Semitism which have bred pogroms at worst, hostile attitudes at best... if Jews were allowed to emigrate or at least travel to other countries, policies permitted by any humane government... if—"

"'If, if, if, if...'" an impatient Svetlova waved his hand as though to wipe away each item on Rabbi Chair's bill of particulars. "I fear, Rabbi Chair, that you have been victimized by a pack of vile falsehoods emanating from the Jewish press of the West, the selfsame bunch of greedy usurers who pour their ill-gotten shekels into the swollen coffers of the artificial Zionist state. Jews of the Soviet Union are content, fulfilled. They are tolerated almost everywhere. They are even to be found in the highest strata of our lower echelons. But we are wasting our time with this fruitless dialogue. One thing is sure—'Operation Matzohball' is blown. I shall see that this wretched house of yours is smoldering on a garbage dump in ten minutes."

"One question, sir," said Rabbi Chair. "Let us go back to your initial belief of my identity as someone other than myself. What is the mystery all about?"

"I may as well tell you, Rabbi, since it will not be helpful to you in any event. Rotten Roger, our enterprising caller, stated that you were the legendary Hebrew superhero who electrified the world with his derring-do in that overglamorized business a year ago. You, of course, recall the affair of the infamous Lazarus Loxfinger."[*]

---

[*] See (and buy) *Loxfinger*, Pocket Books, Inc., 1965, $1, the definitive depiction of espionage.

His eyes widening, the rabbi laughed. "You thought that I, sir, was…"

"Israel Bond," Svetlova cut in. "Or Oy Oy Seven, as he is known to your secret service. It was reported he had died of wounds incurred during the climax of the affair in the Red Sea. We naturally tended to doubt such reports. Yet, you are plainly not he. Perhaps he did, indeed, go to that reeking Jewish heaven of yours and is presently strumming the songs of David upon his golden lyre. Enough exposition, Rabbi Chair. I shall now proceed to crumble Israel's paltry scheme to bits as one crumbles matzoh in one's hand. Too bad; it was a most interesting house. Before I order it razed, why not show me around? A Cook's tour, as our capitalistic friends would call it."

"It would be my pleasure," said Rabbi Chair with a grave smile. "And since it is a Cook's tour, let me make a small pun of my own. A Cook's tour is best begun in the kitchen." And he held the front door open with the studied politeness of an Intourist guide.

"Droll, Rabbi. The kitchen, of course." Svetlova moved quickly about the kitchen, sniffing here and there, breaking off pieces of matzoh from walls, chairs, the table and nibbling them. On one end of the table was a covered dish. He lifted the checkered cloth. "Ah, what is this?"

"Plastic representations of the ethnic foods to be found on a typical Jewish table. See, here is a bottle of Tab. This is lox, the smoked salmon… here is cream cheese… and here," his finger indicated a round varnished object with a hole in its center, "a bagel. Oh please, sir, do not remove it from its base. It is anchored to the dish by a wire, as are all these representations. We did not want visitors to disrupt the display."

"What does it matter now?" asked Svetlova. If it would upset the rabbi to rip the bagel from its moorings, he would do just that. He gave the bagel a violent yank.

A bell rang, shattering the stillness of the deserted street outside the Institute of Architecture.

If one had tried to trace the source of the ringing, one would have been frustrated, indeed, for on this street there were no public telephones or fire-alarm boxes. It was coming from a most unlikely place, the handle of a mop in the hands of one of a pair of shabbily attired women street cleaners, the type to be seen all over Moscow.

"It's the bagel," said the mop wielder in a rich baritone voice.

"Then it's got to be trouble. The bagel only goes off when the wire is severed," answered the other woman in an even deeper bass.

"Let's get the hell in there!" cried the first crone. "It's blown. He's in trouble."

"Hold it! The two gentlemen trying to look so casual near the side entrance... KGB boys, if I ever saw any. I can smell 'em a mile away."

The possessor of the acute olfactory sense was, of course, no woman at all, but Israeli agent Zvi Gates, he of the piercing eyes and the artificial ear.[*] Zvi Gates, 113 in the branch, licensed to wound. Street cleaner Number Two was young, personable Itzhok Ben Franklin, 276, licensed to drive.

Hampered somewhat by their unfamiliar, cumbersome garb, they had slowly moved about the street cleaning the same spots time after time, always keeping the Institute in view. Never had the street, nor the five sleeping drunks they had scrubbed a dozen times, gleamed so. Itzhok had proposed using a liquid cleaner of no mean repute, but Zvi, the older hand, vetoed it. "It's all right for the small jobs, but if you want to do a big job—like a street—you have to dilute it in water and it loses its power. Nah, we'll use something made to be *mixed* in water. Spic & Span."

They began a measured shuffle toward the two Russian goons, Federenko and Norelco, who leaned against the loading platform, puffing strong Gorki Cigarettes with one-inch gork tips.

"*Dobri noch*, gentlemen sirs," said Zvi, bowing obsequiously as a cleaning woman would before her superiors. "My, they are two very handsome gentlemen sirs, are they not, Sonyushkah?"

"*Da*, to be sure," croaked Itzhok, eyes twinkling with allure.

"Be gone, you stinking old carrion!" Federenko commanded. Russian women! Clods they were, clods! Give me a tawny, uninhibited *fräulein* any time, thought Federenko, who had performed many missions in West Berlin. In his mind he revisited Liselotte Gerhardt who had used her passionate teeth to bite her address and phone number into his neck.

"Oh, *nyet*, Nikolai. Not sending them away," pleaded the hassocklike protege of Colonel Svetlova. "They very beautiful

---

[*]   The loss of 113's ear is described in *Loxfinger*, Pocket Books, Inc., 1965, $1, a splendid Chanukah or Christmas gift to promote interfaith understanding. It can also be given to mark Arbor Day, National Blotter and Stylus Week and President Polk's birthday.

women. I not see women so beautiful like these back on farm."
Norelco, a simple-minded field hand, was bursting to experiment
with the strange stirrings that of late had been disturbing his
young body. So far his only experience along those lines had
been a disappointing five minutes in a fetid barn with a bored
cow. A prostitute at that.

"Let them stay if it pleases you, *muzhik,*[*] shrugged Federenko,
shivering as his fingertips tenderly caressed his neck and "56-B
Krupp Strasse, 8765" in reminiscence.

"We clean spot right here, eh, Sonyushkah?" said Zvi. Itzhok
nodded and they set about mixing a powder into the battered
pail of milky water. "Better use strong powder; plenty dirty
pavement here," admonished Itzhok. Zvi poured the powder into
the pail, humming "Moscow Nights," but at the same time he let
slip from under his petticoat a small green cube, crying "Pinch
nose!" The mixture fizzled for a second; then burst into a green
gaseous ball. The two women, forefingers and thumbs squeezing
their noses, held their breaths. Norelco fell forward, his head
striking the side of the platform, blood spurted from a pulsating
fountain of a wound. "A trap!" Federenko screamed. Coughing,
choking, he barreled past the two women into the Institute.

"This piece of matzoh," said Svetlova. "I wrenched it from a
bedroom closet door. It's different from the others." He and his
rabbinical host, the tour at an end, stood in front of the house
watching the floodlights flash rays off its silvery skin.

"Matzoh is matzoh," the rabbi said mildly. "I can't imagine
there being any difference at all."

"Thicker. Yes, definitely thicker. But why?" He began to
knead the fragment in his hand. Crumbs snowed upon his boot
tips. And then something else fell to the floor—a shiny black
sort of ribboned material. He picked it up, held it to the light.
"Microfilm!"

"Ah, yes," said Rabbi Chair. "That, I suspect, would be one of
the microfilms of the holy prayer books, reduced in such a way
that a few rolls contain the entire liturgy."

And suddenly Colonel Svetlova realized that the stoop-
shouldered savant had straightened up. He shoved the rabbi back
with a flailing left hand, dug into his holster for the Walther PPK
Reuther with the right, extricating it with the lightning draw

---

[*]   Peasant.

that had earned him a reputation in the KGB as "the fastest gun in the East."

This time it was not fast enough.

Even as Svetlova shoved him back, Rabbi Chair's right hand made a mercurial maneuver of its own, whipping the yarmulkeh from his head and sailing it at his Soviet guest with the power of an Outback aborigine hurling a boomerang.

Five sounds fought simultaneously for dominance in the Institute of Architecture.

—The frightening, whirring sound of Rabbi Chair's yarmulkeh jetting toward its goal, a short exciting marriage.

—Qang! The marriage: steel-lined yarmulkeh to its eager waiting lover, the steel plate in the head of Colonel Sergei Svetlova.

—*Strike! Strike!* The characteristic sound of the Walther PPK Reuther blazing in the misdirected right hand of the falling KGB bigwig.

—"It's a trap! Tra... !" The gas-blasted, nearly unconscious Nikolai Federenko stumbled onto the scene, a crippled deer with its foreleg shot away.

—His tortured "aaa-eee-iii-ooo-uuu" scream gargling in his throat, torn open by Svetlova's two slugs.

Then, to the rabbi, the sweetest sound he'd ever heard. The sound of silence.

Two men lay on the floor of the Institute of Architecture in slowly widening pools of blood, faces contorted in the attitudes of sudden violent death.

Israel Bond, alias Rabbi Morris Chair, dazedly wiped the coursing streamlets trickling from his brow into his eyes. Sweat, thank God, and nothing more. His Type-A blood had not been shed this time.

He pulled out a crumpled pack of Raleighs from a vest pocket, stuck one into his lips and scratched an Ohio bluetipped match on the door of the house. He let the smoke curl in sensuous spirals out of his mouth, nose, and ears. Footsteps clickclacked behind him, Zvi and Itzhok chugging in still in their old-maidish costumes. The heavy lisle panties had fallen around Zvi's ankles.

"Clean it up, *boochereem*,"[*] said Oy Oy Seven, his famed scar livid on either his left or right cheek, now that his long tapering fingers had stripped away the rubberoid hands and mask that had transformed him into a sexagenarian.

---

[*] A Hebrew word for "boys."

Zvi spoke. "Oy Oy Seven, sorry this one"—he kicked the sole of Federenko's shoe—"got away. Gas got the other, but this guy had a little extra staying power. And our KGB luminary in the tunic... what got him, Bond?"

Zvi, of course, was hurling a challenge at his idol, Oy Oy Seven, whose ability to inject scintillating humor into even the most perilous circumstances was well-known to all his acquaintances. And basically ignored. Except by the jocular Zvi, who loved a hearty joke and always stood like a tittering maiden in the presence of a movie star, awaiting Oy Oy Seven's next gem.

Bond knew this too well. *Gottenu!* he thought; I'm exhausted, enervated. My kingdom for a good Robert Orben jokebook right now. But there's none handy. This'll have to be *my* rib-tickler.

He smiled weakly; threw his Saturday punch. (Bond's commitment to Judaism was an integral part of his make-up.)

"What got Colonel Sergei Svetlova, dear Zvi? He made one fatal mistake. He used his head."

Zvi purpled, a soft wheeze escalated into a howling hurricane of laughter. Slapping his knee, he lost his balance and fell against the point of Federenko's shoe, bloodying his nose. "Used his head! Oh, *mommeleh*, what a mind! Dig, Itzhok? He used his *head!*"

Itzhok said politely, "Oh."

"Okay," grinned a satisfied Bond. "Fun and games over. Get this house dismantled and into the truck. Your contacts are meeting you at the Reese-Schapiro Bridge at midnight. Get cracking!"

As the two younger Israelis loaded the matzoh segments onto the rickety old E. B. White truck, he gave them a brief perceptive rundown on his minutes of torment at the hands of Colonel Svetlova.

Bond glanced down at his fallen foe again, the gash of a mouth congealed into a frozen Z, glazed eyes like bloodshot marbles caught in a ghastly white light. *"Russkoyeh sveenyah, vui!"* Then he looked at the tunic, snapped his fingers.

"Boochereem, they'll be searching high and low for Rabbi Morris Chair for sure. They know—" He cut himself short; he would not bring up the matter of the traitor at this crucial moment in the plot—"uh, I have a feeling they might be looking for the rabbi when the colonel doesn't check back in. But here's

---

* "Russian swine, you!" (A term of dislike.)

my passport out of this Godforsaken people's paradise. His uniform."

"Real Oy Oy thinking, boychikl," enthused Zvi. "Take his papers, his car, the whole schmear. Who the hell will have the guts to stop a KGB titan?"

"Another, bigger KGB titan, you schnook," said Bond with severity. "They'll all be out looking for him, especially General Bolshyeeyit, the section boss. But if I can just grab a plane out of here...."

Minutes later, Bond was resplendent in his borrowed military togs—beard and payis shaved away by Zvi's .22 Remington. The only jarring note was the trouser cuffs which ended at his knees.

"The bodies, Oy Oy Seven," said Zvi. "What about 'em?"

Bond's eyes were mischievous. "Watch, lads. We're going to make the bodies disappear. And as an added fringe benefit, a hundred-million-dollar installation, the Institute of Architecture."

Zvi's eyes blinked. *"Gevaldt! How?"*

Bond picked up the prayer shawl; kissed it reverently. He felt for the fringes on the right side of the shawl, pulled one out to a length of some twenty inches. "The fuse, gentlemen. The entire talis is woven out of explosive *plastique.*"

"HaLavi, huh?" Zvi asked, answering his own question: Lavi HaLavi, quartermaster of M 33 and 1/3, creator of diabolical devices for espionage, such as the yarmulkeh.

"Colonel" Bond lit another safety match, touched it to the elongated fringe. "Let's leave it to the angels, *boochereem,* and get the hell out of here. It's now fifteen minutes to boom time."

He climbed into Svetlova's staff car, pressed the hands of Zvi and Itzhok in fond farewell.

"You know," mused Zvi, "that colonel's suit looks kinda sharp on you, Bond."

Bond smiled. (He'd been saving this bon mot for Zvi.) "Well, I'll tell you, Zvi. I always was crazy about... Russian dressing."

Zvi's body shook convulsively. "Oh, *mommeleh!* I think I wet my pants!"

That Zvi! Bond cackled all the way to the airport, where he was sure he could pull rank and somehow con his way onto a jetliner to the West. Ah, the West! No matter what its faults, it stood out as a bright beacon in the eyes of all free men.

Even as that refreshing metaphor crossed his mind there was a robust Russian answer to that bright beacon. It came as a red flash that split the cold darkness of the Moscow night, accompanied by a thunderous rumble that shattered the windows in Svetlova's 1963 Karamazov sedan.

Bond dragged on a Raleigh. "Well, there goes the Institute. Even Frank Lloyd couldn't put that building Wright!"

And desperately wished Zvi could have been there to hear *that* one.

4
"There Will Be No Third Striking"

Rumors flew like U-2's around Moscow concerning the explosion and fiery destruction of the Institute of Architecture. The Red Chinese were the culprits, seeking revenge for the latest Politbureau blast at Mao Tse-tung, some claimed. Others pinned the disaster on counterrevolutionary elements trying to overturn the Soviet regime and place Anastasia back on the throne. A CIA job. Albanian terrorists. Rasputin—no one in Russia believed he had really died. Ayn Rand practicing her own philosophy.

To A. Schlepin, shadowy security chieftain of the Soviet Union, General Bolshyeeyit had been compelled to tell the truth, at least *his* version. "He deserved to die, the stupid glory seeker," said Bolshyeeyit, "tackling a man like this Israeli with only himself and two others."

"Nevertheless, General, we have suffered a humiliating defeat: the matzoh is on its way; three of our men are dead. KGB's morale has been shattered to the breaking point. We must have a stunning victory immediately. That is an order."

From the glacial quality of the interview Bolshyeeyit knew he must improvise a way back to Schlepin's good graces at once.

"Comrade Minister," he began guardedly. "What... what if KGB could revenge itself upon the Zionist state for this outrage?"

"How, General, without admitting to the world that little Israel was able to wreak an act of monumental havoc upon the proud Russian bear in the very heart of his capital?"

"True," Bolshyeeyit nodded. "But the world at large does not know of Israel's daring. Perhaps our world, the world of intelligence, knows by now, and it is that world we can impress, by destroying the very Israeli who was the death instrument of Svetlova, and the bomber in the Institute job."

"Israel Bond," Schlepin gave a cool, reflective blow on his pipe, sending the bubbles on an upside-down pyramid to the ceiling. And Bolshyeeyit knew he had temporarily saved his spurs by the spark of interest in the minister's eye.

"Israel Bond," Bolshyeeyit echoed. "Think of our restored, even enhanced, prestige when the great intelligence bureaus of the world —America's CIA, England's M.I. 5, the French Surete, Netherland's KLM—learn that KGB has brought down the great secret agent at the height of his gaudy career."

"How would they know it was KGB's handiwork?" "Easily arranged, Comrade Minister. As you know, there was recently opened in Lisbon... 'The Espionage Capital of the World' as its Chamber of Commerce proudly states on its letterheads... a new hotel, the Hilton Spy, whose clientele consists solely of undercover agents. I myself have spent a relaxing weekend in its Colonel Rudolph Abel Suite, which, of course, has red carpets. Now... what if someday the famed killing mezuzah of Israel Bond was tacked upon the bulletin board in the lobby for all spies to gape at in awe, with a message beneath: 'From Russia With You Know What. Let This Be a Warning to All Who Would Harm the Soviet Union.'"

"I see the merit of your proposal," Schlepin remarked. "But I tell you, General Bolshyeeyit: this is your last chance to redeem yourself. If Israel Bond is not destroyed...." his hands made a gesture conveying finality. "Our American friends have a proverb derived from their national pastime—basketbowling, is not? They say, 'Three strikings and you are a dugout.'"

"There will be no third striking," responded Bolshyeeyit, whose knowledge of Americana was easily as comprehensive as his chieftain's.

"What will be your death instrument? I am told that Professor Gletkin of our weapons research division has concocted a particularly agonizing poison cigarette."

"It will not work on this man, Comrade Minister. His dossier indicates he has been smoking an American brand called Raleigh for many years. No, I shall employ Israel Bond's greatest enemy against him, one that lurks within the confines of that lithe muscular body. Sex. German measles has not attacked as many women as he has. Sex will be our death instrument against Israel Bond."

5
The Tender Teach-in

At the precise moment General Bolshyeeyit was outlining his plan for retaliation, Bond, a strange softness on that dark, cruelly handsome visage, was gazing fondly upon the innocence of an oval feline face, running a forefinger across the pouting baby mouth.

They were the property of Rowena Rosenthal, blonde and eighteen, who slept trustingly in his arms on the superior Beautyrest mattress ("Reminds me of a best seller," he had jested as he took her, *"The Silent Spring"*) which cushioned the oxblood-stained Belmar, New Jersey, driftwood bed in his luxury suite at New York City's opulent Ansonia Hotel.

An hour ago, fresh off the London-to-New York BOAC super fanjet, his tension-triggered perspiration blown away by the gentle fans, Bond had restively prowled Manhattan's upper 90's in search of *divertissement,* some escapade to blot out the unbearable strain from his grim sojourn in the Soviet Union. Dressed with expensive casualness in a Rudi Gernreich coral-tinted burlap-weave suit, Esquire socks held up by sporty *TV Guide* garters, Lazy Possum hush puppies by Thom McAn which squeaked Nina Simone songs as he walked, V-taper Jimmy Van Heusen shirt with the white-on-white musical note pattern and a clip-on Franklin Pangborn paisley bowtie, he sauntered up Broadway. He considered taking in a movie; there were several small cinema palaces in the area. The Thalia's marquee advertised Walt Disney's *Harlow,* about the fifth or sixth filmic attempt at capturing the true meaning of the tempestuous sex goddess' life. And the best so far, according to one critic, since it was a full-length cartoon. The Symphony was exhibiting a horror masterpiece, one of a number of such vehicles starring the screen idols of the 1930's who were making comebacks in films of a macabre vein. The new shocker was *Die! Die! Good Ship Lollipop!*, starring Shirley Temple as the deranged host of a kiddie television show who plastered the little tykes' faces with lye pies. The twinbill at the Midtown held no appeal at all: *I Passed for White*, with Ossie Davis, a truly splendid actor, miscast terribly as a substitute quarterback who comes off the bench with 1:09 left to lead Rockne's Fighting Irish (played by William Buckley and the Yale varsity of 1921) over Southern California, with his aerial bombs; and its cofeature, a science-fiction potboiler about a mutant three-hundred-foot rye bread that escapes from the kitchens of Jennie Grossinger to terrorize the world, *The Beast That Came From the Yeast*.

He stopped at a newsstand for his copy of the spicy, informative *National Enquirer* (the lead story this week blared: "I CHOPPED MY MOTHER INTO A THOUSAND BITS AND SPRINKLED HER OVER MY WALDORF SALAD"), and a pack of Raleighs. "Sure you wouldn't like to come on over to the L & M side, Mr. Bond?" said affable proprietor Don Dewsnap, offering him a snowy filter-tipped smoke.

"Sorry, Don," he grinned back. "Not until they give me coupons with 'em." Would that he could have told him, "Don, there are four hundred Mystery jets sweeping all hostile invaders from the skies of my beloved Eretz Israel. That kind of hardware doesn't come for free, Don. Each jet costs my plucky little nation three million coupons."

Then he had strolled into an espresso joint on 96th Street, The Maxwell House, unofficial hangout of America's new radical left. There he had met the fetching Rowena and her boisterous claque at the bar as they exulted over their latest triumph, the desegregation of a previously all-white house of prostitution on Lexington Avenue. "We did it!" she cried. "Made 'em take their first CORE whore!"

She had rejected Bond's initial advances after a sullen size-up: "We new yoot of America frankly distrust anybody over thirty. You're Establishment, *status quo*, smug mugwumps, bourgeois liberals... sell us out every time." Master of improvisation that he was, Bond had baited a clever trap using her own jargon. He lured her to his suite under the pretext that he was going to conduct a "teach-in."

Once there, all pedagogical pretense was abandoned. Ripping away her faded jeans, bra and panties, all of blue denim, and her Patrice Lumumba T-shirt, he crushed his cruel sensual mouth to hers, steering her into a dizzying orbital swing among the stars of fulfillment.

Rowena aslumber in the crook of his muscular arm, Raleigh smoke filtering through alert, vigilant nasal hairs, he recalled the events that had plunged him into that heartland of intrigue, Soviet Russia.

"Operation Matzohball" had been one of two schemes handed to the strategy board of M 33 and 1/3 by HaLavi. The alternate, "Operation Reunion," a brazen bid to spirit away all of Russia's Jews, had been scrubbed by M. "There is, I fear, no Russian highway, nor any other," M. had said wisely, "that can accommodate a three-mile wide, four-mile long bus." But "Matzohball" had won M.'s top priority. "Russia's Jews sorely need an injection of the Jewish feeling. Without some sign of external concern they could well become as spiritually destitute as the Jews of America and Israel. There is only one man with the leonine courage to spearhead this mission. Bond. I am told his shoulder and hand wounds are healed."

Bond had undergone a grinding program of physical training, running six miles a day across the golden beaches of Ashkelon on the Mediterranean under the watchful eye of frail peach-whiskered Nochum Spector, a nephew of M., who held a minor code clerk's post in the service. Healing sunlight had bronzed that pale bullet-gouged body once more; applications of Mother Margolies' Activated Old World Chickenfat had toned the skin, and selected isometric exercises, the diligent pitting of one muscle against another, had given him new strength and elasticity—and pitted muscles. Evenings he spent with the real Rabbi Morris Chair, polishing up his cover role, copying the sage's stooped stance, gentle speech and self-effacing gestures. His beard and forelocks had grown at an amazing rate, the result of hormones injected nightly by Dr. Lewis Hirsh, trail blazer in accelerated hair growth. It was jokingly reported the doctor's preparation could grow hair on billiard balls. Bond, shooting a little friendly game of snooker in the doctor's gameroom one night, could attest to that. The pockets of the table were jammed with hirsute spheroids that would not go down.

HaLavi's final touches. "You must work this job 'clean,' Oy Oy Seven. Your mezuzah weapon must be left at home. I'm sure it is no secret to Soviet intelligence anymore. If you are frisked its discovery will uncover your cover. You'll wear a real one. The same logic, I'm sorry to say, applies to your heel knives. Regular shoes, Bond. Your eyes will be changed to brown by contact lenses; an old trick, but we will add a refinement. Two strands of that beard will in actuality be wires attached to tiny ducts at the side of each eye. If some playful Russian gives your impressive bush a pull, fluid will be released. Your eyes will weep."

"But, Lavi," Bond said ruefully, "I'll be entirely without weapons. I don't know what's waiting for me out in the field. Whatever it is I can't face it defenseless. Remember, I am licensed to kill."

Thus, the QM had relented, fashioned the *plastique* talis and the killing skullcap with its hidden rim of razor-sharp Swedish steel.

Finally the big night had come, the confrontation with Svetlova. Thank God for his insistence on weapons and the creative powers of HaLavi!

At the airport he had arrogantly shoved his way aboard a British European Airlines jet for London, bumping off one Fedya Zhivago, an osteopathic veterinarian, who had quailed at the flashed KGB card and gratefully fled the plane. All during the flight he had played the overbearing no-nonsense role of the colonel to the teeth, slipping just once when the overawed passenger next to him had timidly ventured, "Comrade Colonel, you must be very proud of that red star on your uniform. Who presented it to you?" Bond, his mind elsewhere, had answered: "Texaco." His eyes had peered into the velvety blue, picking out from the myriads of stars the constellation known as the Big Dipper, a pattern of celestial bodies which, when connected by the imaginary line of the mind, formed the face of Wilt Chamberlain.

Then a bump... the jet's wheels caressed the free soil of Great Britain. At the airport with a change of clothes was Judah Ben Gay, a British liniment manufacturer who also happened to be 456 in the service, licensed to rub. And a dash for the BOAC jet and, six hours later, New York.

Rowena moaned, stirred in his arms. "I'm naked."

"You're very observant," said Bond, his lips curved into a suave, humorous smile.

"Who are you?" she said incuriously, rubbing the sleep from her Booth-hazel eyes. "Oh, yes," a worldly wise smile on the baby mouth. "The teach-in. M-m-m... it was... enlightening. I think I'll go for sixteen more credits." Her plump arms pulled him down to the rose garden of her body. Bond, ever the green thumber, took it from there.

Rebellious, but a wonderful kid, he thought, as she hurried away to start a rent strike at the Essex House (where she lived). He would stop in at the Gene Baylos Boutique and have them send Rowena a little token of his affection, perhaps one of their charming hand-tooled pot-holders. He was certain she smoked it.

He slipped into his Ralston lounging robe, the colorful checkerboard square pattern set off tastefully by a Timmie Rogers "Oh Yeah" ascot, let his electric toothbrush play over his firm, even white teeth and rich red gums. Then a five-second session with the latest oral appliance, Westinghouse's new electric toothpick which deftly ferreted out the insidious particles between those dazzling molars. He was finishing his third gargle with new improved Listerine, relishing the dying screams of a million throat bacteria, when the phone burred.

"Long distance, Mr. Bond," squeaked the hotel's operator, Miss Gloria Halfon, who was fascinated by Bond but too shy to make any overtures beyond leaving a nude photo of herself in his mailbox. "Tel Aviv, Israel, calling. Mother Margolies on the line."

Mother Margolies? Calling direct? His steely left fist clenched, the Speidel watchband snapping off in his anxiety. It was unthinkable of Mother to make a personal call unless a Code 3-D condition existed—Danger-Doom-Disaster! It signified to any truly astute Israeli "op" that something was amiss.

Mother Emma Margolies, known to an adoring humanity as the kindly wise soul of eighty-one golden years whose renowned cooking (Betty Crocker asked *her* for recipes) was savored by lipsmacking gourmets from somewhere east of Suez to China 'crost the bay. Her celebrated chicken soup graced the elegant tables of presidents, kings, Indian rajahs, British rock 'n' roll stars. Yes, she was everybody's Jewish mother (even Dan Greenberg's), dispensing equal dosages of gastronomic delights and straight-from-the-heart proverbs of universal understanding, such as: "You can't teach an old dog new tricks. But you *can* teach an old dog to teach a young dog *old* tricks." (Pundits of every major religion and philosophy were still probing for the inner meaning of that one; only the Dalai Lama was even close.) Once

she had whispered to the American ambassador at a glittering
state reception: "Remember, mine dear Yankee—the enemy of
my enemy is my enemy's enemy." Bond himself had felt a catch
in his throat when Mother had once remarked after his return
from a hazardous outing: "Live each day as though it were your
last because, if it really turns out to be your last, you will have
made it last as long as a last day can last." He had gleaned most
of the import of those words; only the last part had thrown him.

Yes, this was her image to everyone but the little band of
brothers who comprised M 33 and 1/3, the men and women
who slithered in the dark jungle of espionage. They knew her as
M., Number One! She had allocated a small wing of her chicken
soup factory for their nefarious activities. There they schemed,
trained for mortal combat with their hostile Arab neighbors,
conceived idealistic operations such as the one he had just
completed.

"*Shalom,* Oy Oy Seven," her voice pierced the crackling static
of the overseas cable. "How was your Slavic interlude?"

"The sale was transacted. However, three directors of the
rival company were taken off the board. And one of their
factories was destroyed."

"So I have been reading in the Moscow papers. Unfortunate."

"I must inform the office that one of our salesmen has
been wooed away by the rival firm. He has been selling them
information about next year's line."

In Tel Aviv, Mother sucked on a piece of rock candy clamped
in her dentures; sipped, from a glass hot tea at her elbow. A
traitor! "Who is the unethical salesman?"

Bond bit on the Raleigh between his own teeth. "I cannot say.
But I feel he is one of the sales task force which accompanied me
to Moscow. We can better discuss this problem when I return
home for the first Passover Seder night, five days hence."

"I am sorry to disappoint you, Mr. Bond. A distressing
sales problem has come up in our branch office at Station WI.
Detailed information will be available from Ben Bon Ami, whose
address may be found in the Spanish edition of our catalogue.
There is a plane leaving tomorrow at 8 A.M. from JFK. On it will
be the other three members of your 'Matzohball' team—Gates,
Franklin, Spector. You will need all the assistance you can get.
And, perhaps during the course of your next enterprise, you can
unearth the identity of our unethical salesman. *Shalom...* and

remember the fool plays his cards close to his vest, but the wise man has a marked deck and five aces *under* his vest."

Long after M. had rung off Bond stood silent, his handsome dark face caught up by a frown of deep concentration. Rotten luck! This Passover would find him far from his beloved Israel, involved in heaven alone knew what kind of assignment, the whole mess compounded by a queasy feeling that one of his teammates was a turncoat. Well, that was an Oy Oy agent's lot, danger and double-dealing. Don't go soft, Bond, he sneered at himself. It's got to be done. Now let's look at the Spanish edition and find out where we're heading.

From a thick black Spanish "catalogue" titled "Soup y Sales" he extracted a slim pamphlet hidden in the binding and unrolled it. His fingers skimmed the contents. "Station WI." The West Indies. Under that category he found the name Ben Bon Ami, 41 Cinco de Finko, Vera Hruba.

Vera Hruba! Good God! The capital city of the sinkhole of the world! Israel Bond was going to the pestilential, revolution-racked, murder-ridden Caribbean island of—El Tiparillo!

6
Rotten Roger:
The Second Call

Even General Bolshyeeyit's favorite program on Soviet TV, *The Man From UNCLE Vanya*, could not erase what had been a most distasteful day for him.

To begin with, he had sweated through his monthly tryst with Sergeant Treshkova, a sickening, teeth-grinding affair as always, consummated in the back of a covered Red Army lorry at 2 A.M. since he would not permit her to be seen with him in decent society during daylight. The thought of her harelip pressed greedily against his mouth caused him to shudder. And her harsh voice cooing, "Say pretty things to me, my dear General lover... tell me I am lovely...." *Bozheh moy!* Yet it was a necessity. Money could not tempt her to perform the vital chores he required from her from time to time, things he could not trust any of his other underlings to do. In her case, love was the key that opened the door to snooping, listening, reporting. But how he wished that her lock would be satiated by another key!

And headache Number Two, a call from Minister Schlepin:

"What has happened to your campaign to rid us of this dirty *Zhid,*[*] Israel Bond? I am growing impatient, General."

"It is progressing nicely," said General Bolshyeeyit. "Already my agent is on the way to make contact with him." A blatant lie. The general had no idea where Bond could be at the moment; his world-wide alert to all full-time agents and stringers had not uncovered the Israeli's whereabouts.

In this irritable frame of mind he had exploded when the timid switchboard operator said, "A thousand pardons, General,

[*] Jew.

but I have a long distance call from a person who is not on the master list of those permitted to get through to you. Yet he claims he has highly significant information for you and you alone...."

"You stupid bitch! How dare you bother me with crank calls! I shall have you tortured, shot, hung from Chapaiyev's statue...."

He was just about to hang up when he heard her sobbing voice say, "I am sorry, Gospideen Colfax. The general cannot be—"

"Wait!" he thundered, then tried to soften his voice. "I have been a little harsh... unnecessarily, Comrade Ponyebratzie. I shall take the call." Fool that I am! He thumped his brow in self-anger. Colfax! The very man who might extricate me from this mess.

"This is General Bolshyeeyit."

"General, this is Rotten Roger Colfax. I have some information which may be of use to you. But this time it will cost you."

"How much, Gospideen Colfax?"

"One million rubles. To be delivered by tomorrow. It must be left with a Dr. Nu at the Temple of Hate on El Tiparillo. Your people on that unhappy island will know of the establishment. If it is delivered, I shall call many more times with tasty items... at a price, of course."

Bolshyeeyit, a man used to making decisions of paramount importance in a hurry, said, "I accept your terms. The money will be there, I promise you. Now, what is the information you have now?"

"By now you have guessed that I am attached to M 33 and 1/3. I was part of the band that perpetrated the killing of your colonel and his two aides and the blowing up of your Institute. The leader of that strike was Israel Bond, our beloved secret agent here."

Was that apposition cast in a sarcastic vein? This man must have a personal vendetta against Bond. It can be highly useful to me.

"Where is Bond now?"

"He leaves 8 A.M. tomorrow, New York time, on Southeast Accident Airlines. The plane will make a stop at Miami at 10:14 A.M., also New York time. Since that airline does not go to El Tiparillo, he will be compelled to take the only line that services the island, Tailspin Tannenbaum's Flying Aardvark Airways. It leaves at 9 A.M., Miami time, the following day."

"I am most grateful for that information, Gospideen Colfax. Am I correct in assuming that any... uh... misfortune that Bond might incur would not displease you a great deal?"

"You are."

"Excellent. I have assigned a very beautiful courier to arrange for the misfortune. Now, how can I contact you for further data?"

"You may leave word at the Temple of Hate. *Dosvedanyah,* General." And Rotten Roger signed off.

General Bolshyeeyit pounded his fist into his palm. *"Chorosho!*[*] There is time. It will be close, but there is time. Israel Bond, prepare to meet your maker."

---

[*] Russian for "good"; like many Russian words and phrases, constant repeating of these guttural sounds can be useful in clearing your sinuses.

7
The Eyes And Thighs
Of A Fawn

In the speeding cab to Kennedy, Bond sorted through the mail that had piled up in his box at the Ansonia. Most of it the usual junk mail.... "You may have already won an evening with Lenny Bruce or Pearl Williams in the Imperial Margarine Date-A-Dream Contest".... "The Schlockmeister Organization is a progressive mutual funds agency which takes what it deems to be sensible risks in purchasing only the most promising blue-sky stock".... and that accursed rejection from the cartoon book syndicate: "We feel that your idea does not have the general appeal, etc."

Stupid, shortsighted bastards! He had thrown a multimillion-dollar bonanza in their gray-flannel laps and they had been too myopic to realize its value. Some months ago he had suggested that since they were already making stupendous profits with Superman and Superboy, why not go all the way and milk the idea from its logical beginning? "The new character would be called Supersperm, the adventures of Superman from the moment of conception," he had written. "Surely, even then there must have been all sorts of hair-raising episodes in the womb for the Sperm of Steel. Think of the possibilities, gentlemen! The doughty infinitesimal dot, clad in red cape and blue leotards, fighting off hosts of fanatical germs launched by Luthor, the Mad Spirochete! Supersperm refereeing a race to the death in the stomach between Anacin, Bufferin and aspirin! Supersperm battling the swollen yellow forces of cholesterol in a last-ditch effort to keep his mother's arteries...."

The hell with it! he thought bitterly.

An accent textured with thick Brooklynese broke the silence. The cab driver. "You know, buddy, I ride around dese here streets all day, meetin' all kinds of people; some rich, some poor, some black, some white, some tall, some short. And, you know, buddy, I kinda developed me own philosophy on duh vicissitudes of life."

Gottenu! thought Bond, another hackie-philosopher. Spare me, Lord. "What's your name, my good man?"

"Friedrich Nietzsche."

Perhaps, Bond mused, this man would be worth listening to. But now there was no time for timelessness. Ahead lay JFK Airport and the Southeast Accident superliner for Miami. He wisely tripled the amount of his flight insurance naming Mother Margolies as his principal beneficiary, with ten per cent allocated to the Espionage Tzeddukah Charity Fund, set up to provide black mink coats for the grief-stricken widows of Israeli operatives.

He sat watching the trucks pump the enriched Humble Company gasoline into the plane's hungry tanks. An odd name for a Texas product, he reflected. In his many visits to the Lone Star State he had never found anything even remotely humble.

On his way to the first-class Golden Circle area he spotted Zvi, Itzhok and Nochum but professionally gave them no glance of recognition. They were ensconced in the twelve-seat-across tourist section, appearing somewhat cramped and unhappy. Rank hath its privileges, he admitted. An Oy Oy holder deserved the luxurious touches befitting his station. Golden Circle travelers dined on Sea Isle, Georgia, pheasant under Chagall stained glass, swigged chilled Jive 7 wine in ice buckets, served by bright-eyed slinky stewardesses in crisp topless uniforms. For the tourist crowd it was a box of Nabisco fignewtons and orange Kool-Ade, served by hostesses who looked like Blanche Yurka.

Yes, there they sat... Zvi, Itzhok, Nochum, three lads who had helped him tweak the nose of the Russian bear. He could not believe even now that one of them was the traitorous Rotten Roger Colfax. Which one?

Zvi and Itzhok had done the lugging and the strong-arm work; Nochum had acted as liaison and kept in constant telephonic contact with the main office. Telephone! He could have been the caller! But then, any one of them could have stolen a moment to buzz Svetlova.

What did he know of them anyway? Zvi, Jake-of-all-trades, master of disguises, who had joined M 33 and 1/3 several years ago. He knew Zvi longed for a higher designation than 113. "You get all the glamorous assignments, Oy Oy Seven," Zvi had once jested. Was he insanely jealous deep down? And would such envy impel him to treachery? Zvi Gates with his artificial ear,[*] a tragedy caused by Bond's carelessness. Could that have triggered a resentment which turned to all-consuming hatred?

Itzhok Ben Franklin, a new appointee. He doesn't chortle at my rapid-fire jokes. That certainly makes him suspect, The young *Sabra* (native-born Israeli) was a taciturn sort; he was, Bond knew, an honor graduate of the Technion Institute, which turned out Israeli's scientific brain power. Did he consider the low-grade chores allotted to him beneath his intellectual merit?

And Nochum, M.'s nephew, a laughable elf who had failed miserably in a succession of difficult government posts so, thanks to the intercession of his aunt, he had been placed in intelligence. He had more than once begged, "Please, Oy Oy Seven, teach me to kill and grab broads and order food just like you do!" Bond had snickered. "Nochum, stay safe in the playpen. This game is for big boys." Perhaps I was thoughtless at the time. Would that remark have turned Nochum against me and Eretz Israel?

He became conscious of a rustling in the next seat, a pair of astonishing legs sheathed in Lady Damita Jo hose, followed them up past taut thighs, a bewitchingly tucked-in waist, two full jutting breasts straining to liberate themselves from a satiny-black Tuesday Weld-model bra, to a face... and what a face! Piquant, amusing, with two ebony eyes dit-dotting an unmistakable SOS for SEX. Hands smooth, ringless, fingernails tinted tastefully with Revlon's new Annette Funicello pudgy-pink shade. The hair, also ebony, in a chic Shetland pony tail, neatly tied with a Pabst Blue Ribbon.

"Hello-o-o-o," he began. A traditional opener; he'd play it by ear. "Traveling together, are we?"

"We are on the same aircraft. It is a distinct possibility."

There's a keen mind to go with that loveliness! "May I introduce myself?"

---

[*] Once, after the accident which is described in *Loxfinger* (Pocket Books, Inc., 1965, $1, and well worth purchasing), he had said to Bond, "Look at my new ear, Oy Oy Seven. You can hardly tell it from the real article." And Bond, flashing a light into the ear and spotting the drum, had riposted: "Gee, dad, a Wurlitzer!"

"You may as well. I can't do it for you."

Another flash of wit! I could, he told himself, fall in love with a girl like this in twenty seconds. "My name is Bond. Israel Bond."

"Mine is Connery. Fawn Connery." And she glanced at her watch, mumbling "eighteen, nineteen, twenty. Kiss me."

Four lips (divided fairly, evenly between them) fused in a searing instant outside the boundaries of mortal time and space. One of Bond's gold inlays slipped like a molten stream down his windpipe.

Jet motors vibrating, the swan neck of Fawn Connery in the crook of his bronze muscular arm, Israel Bond stared vacantly at the earth below. Already the houses were beginning to look like cigar boxes (they were actually, the plane had not taken off yet). But, finally, up it went, soaring over Long Island, Northern New Jersey, Camden in South Jersey (his eyes picked out the huge sign atop the Campbell's Soup Factory: THIS IS THE HOME OF POP ART) and now they were hurtling southward at five-hundred-and-thirty-five nautical knots per unit of Greenwich median time.

"Is it possible that just one... ?"

"Yes," she said. "It is love. Order me something to eat."

He beckoned for the stewardess, pinched her buttocks and began to order breakfast for two. "We'll both have," he said, a trained eye scanning the menu, "the *filet* of Neolite sole, medium burnt, with a dash of lekvar *flambé*, two strips of Spam, the dark meat only, from selected Iowa corn-fed Poland China sows, titmouse à la Benedictine on Hollywood Diet bread, the bread of all trim figure-conscious stars, and—uh—I think just a smidgen of the poached raven. Suit you, Fawn?"

"Sounds super," she said. It was good to be with a man who knew how to order confidently for a lady without stammering like a schoolboy.

"And we'll share a bottle of Napoleon Solo Brandy. I've always preferred the '38, don't you?"

"The '38," she smiled and found herself running gossamer-winged fingertips across his lean navel. This, she knew, was a man.

"What brings you aboard, my sweet?" Bond probed.

"Oh, business in Miami. Then a vacation on El Tiparillo."

The gray eyes narrowed. "What in God's name would a lovely thing like you do on El Tiparillo? The whole island is sheer madness."

"Maybe I need a little sheer madness," she whispered. "Your kind, Bond." Her hand again skipped across his groin; a kidney stone shattered into powder.

"There'll be a long layover in Miami before tomorrow's plane to El Tiparillo, my Fawn with the fawn eyes. Enough time for a long layover, if I've made myself clear," he said huskily.

"I just might buy it, Israel."

Midnight, read the hands of the Baby Westclox cooing in its layette on the bureau of Room 1818 at Miami Beach's Palmetto Roach Hotel. She lay naked, her lips brushing those of the sleeping Israel Bond with butterfly kisses. She looked at the bronzed body which, melded with her own, had taken them flying to the moon where they played among the stars. She recalled with bitterness the other men she had known, piggish sweaty clods such as Colonel Svetlova, General Bolshyeeyit and the rest. How they had used her as a man uses a tissue, crushes it and throws it into a litter basket! Never had any of them struck the spark that releases the fecundity of a woman. But this man, this wonderful man, the man she had pledged to destroy, he had cracked open wide the dam in the reservoir of her being. And she realized with stark frightening ecstasy in his arms that she had enough within her to irrigate the Gobi Desert.

I do believe this wonderful fool is in love with me, she thought. True, he is a killer; yet there is a boyish quality of trust on his cruel face that tells me he cares. I'm trembling, she thought. A man has made me tremble! And *Bozheh moy!* he is the man I must kill!

From her handbag she took a tube of lipstick and twisted it. Out slid the cosmetic. She had only to press it between those sensual lips and he would die of cyanide poisoning in a few seconds. Her hand moved slowly, closer to the lips of Israel Bond.

"No!" Was that her own voice screaming? "I can't kill you! I can't!"

Bond was now an uncoiled spring; his body lanced out, hand tearing into his jacket for the tiny Paul Derringer. He stopped. Her face was cupped in her hands; an anguished moan heaved her breasts. "I—I can't kill you. I love you, Bond."

He put two Raleighs into his lips, torched the ends of both with a waxy Mexican match which he ignited with a sweep across her buttocks. "Take one now, voyager."

Still snuffling, she inhaled gratefully.

"Now," he began coldly. "Let us have the facts. Obviously you are not a simple vacationer. You were sent to kill me. By whom? And how?"

"KGB," she whimpered. "And with this." She handed him the lipstick, looking away.

He sniffed it; made a grimace. "Cyanide!" And smirked: "The true lover's bouquet."

"You will not believe this, but I love you. I loved you from the moment I sat beside you on the plane, the moment you ordered my *filet* of Neolite sole, the moment you entered my body with your curious admixture of brutishness and tenderness." She looked away from those gray eyes. "You slept serenely, my love. I could have inserted the lipstick at any time."

"True," he acknowledged. "But is this perhaps a ploy to gain my further confidence, Fawn... or whatever your real name is?"

"It is Anna Annatevkah, Corporal, to be precise, acting under the express orders of General Bolshyeeyit who has vowed to repay you for that episode in Moscow. Oh, you fool!" The tears streamed anew. "Can you not see that in betraying my cause I have sealed my own death warrant? I was to have called him tonight with the news of my completed mission."

"Forgive me, Anna," he said, holding her next to a heart moistened by a woman's tears. "I have existed so long in this dirty game that I tend to forget people have true feelings. And now, if you are recovered somewhat, may I offer you a little B & T?"

"B & T?"

"Brutishness and tenderness, dear heart."

Eyes ashine, she whispered, "Yes, oh yes. Oh yes!"

And the Bondian moon rocket tensed again and zoomed them into Orbit Two.

Now the Baby Westclox said 7 A.M. Its functional face watched Bond and Anna, carrying their luggage, leave Room 1818 for the airport. The Israeli looked at the room door for a second; the ghost of a memory etched a faint smile on his lips. It was in this very room a year ago he had courted death and a sinewy Oriental charmer, Nu Kee.[*] This memory had drawn him back to boniface Schuyler Kahn's Palmetto Roach Hotel after he had first checked in with Fawn at the Fontainebleau. But they had not found their room conductive to love-making; the sight of the naked dead girl on the bed, covered from head to toe with gold paint, had all but dampened their flaming urge. So it was back to Mr. Kahn's pink-and-brown stucco pleasure palace. "Glad to see you back, Mr. Bond," the portly little owner had beamed. Poor Kahn, it developed, was having his problems with a new hotel across the street, Horowitz's Hidalgo Hacienda. Seeking to lure Kahn's patrons away, unscrupulous Horowitz had started an odious rumor that sharks had been sighted in Kahn's Olympic-sized swimming pool.

Holding hands like two prom daters, Bond and Anna huddled in the cab, their bodies brushing as it zigzagged its way along Arthur Godfrey Road, Jackie Gleason Drive, and Belle Barth Alley. He caught her peeking at the twinkling new garnet ring in its delicate Freestone peachstone setting setting on her third finger left hand. And they matched the warm contented smiles of lovers who have pledged eternal vows. He had procured it for her from Ben Melzer, a chum of his who handled only the choicest of semiprecious stones. "Damn near a tenth of a carat, darling," he said with pardonable pride. "Only reason Bennie gave it to me so cheap is because it's got a flaw—but he says it's a *perfect* flaw."

Then the reality of their situation came back to him. "You mentioned danger to yourself, Anna."

Those dark eyes clouded. "The general surely will send another 'courier,' Israel. That is why I must go to El Tiparillo with you, to spot him, to warn you in time. I know well the faces of all his henchmen." She hugged him impulsively. I will protect this man at the cost of my own life.

---

[*] See Chapter One of *Loxfinger* (Pocket Books, Inc., 1965, $1, and well worth the price. A thoughtful and well appreciated *Bar Mitzvah* present, or gift to a dying enemy.)

8
Rotten Roger:
The Third Call

"She... she is in love with him?"

The voice at the other end in Miami was venomous. "Of course! She cannot keep her hands off that athletic body. You disappoint me, General Bolshyeeyit. Did you think that any woman could be immune to the blandishments of our Hebrew Hercules? No, General, Oy Oy Seven has literally balled up your works. And your works loves it. But here they come. Good-bye, General. On to El Tiparillo!"

And Rotten Roger Colfax clicked off again.

Bolshyeeyit gnashed his teeth; brought a fist down upon his desk, upsetting an inkwell. "Treshkova, you pig, clean up this mess!" And he flung the heavy glass fixture into her face.

"Oh!" she cried. "My General wants to make love to his adoring Toma again!"

A bullet nicked her skull and she decided, no, this was not the propitious moment.

The hawk-face hardened into a look of hideous hatred. Anna! In the arms of this *Zhid*, willingly yielding every inch of her tantalizing, throat-catching magnificence to this... *Bozheh moy!*

He screamed over the intercom. "Treshkova! Bring me the complete A-file at once, you monstrosity!"

She reappeared; tearfully placed a bulging folder before him.

Despite his shock, he had retained some of his professionalism. If my love-smitten corporal is his concubine now she will recognize my next messenger of death; she will warn him. This will have to be handled by a man outside KGB. In the A-file (A for

Assassins) would be such a cold-blooded kill-for-hire individual, one who sold his murderous talents to the highest bidder.

He leafed through the file. "Niles Gillingham-Pishtepple, forty-eight, ex-British colonel in the Ahmsopur detachment... cashiered out of the service in 1953 for cheating at Old Maid... developed a hatred of the British upper class... offered his services to Communist China in 1954... worked with a renegade kangaroo smuggling out documents in the latter's diplomatic pouch... assassinated pro-British Rajah of Cooch-Dancer by placing botulinus virus in royal swimming tank... comment by investigating officer: 'Dirty pool.'" He saw a footnote: "Gillingham-Pishtepple was shot to death in 1962 by an incensed Outer Mongolian merchant, Hee No Khan Do, leader of the Arctic Secret Society, the Ice Tong, who discovered him trying to erect hotels on Community Chest in a Monopoly game."

Bolshyeeyit, as noted before, a man used to making key decisions with the snap of a finger, said to himself: "He won't do."

Within five minutes he had weeded out all potential assassins, save one. "Of course! This is the only one worthy of consideration. This defection of Anna's has rattled me, else I would have gone to him from the start. Sergeant," he said in a softer tone. "Wipe the blood from your misshapen skull and tell me what you think of this man."

She looked at the documents. For the first time in his recollection he saw her blanch.

"*Da,* Comrade General. He is your man. May I say that truthfully I pity his victim. I would pity anyone, no matter what his crime, whose path crosses that of Torquemada LaBonza."

9
"The Silent One"
Strikes

"Here is your money, *Señor,* ten thousand *habaneras;* your passport and photographs of the man and woman you are to kill. She is one of ours who has defected. He is an Israeli secret agent. The general requests that you remove the religious symbol from his neck after it is done and present it to me here a week hence as proof of your success. Are you clear as to your mission?"

The swarthy man in the flamboyant purple- and yellow-hued gypsy costume nodded. With fastidiousness he smoothed out the thick roll of bills; placed them into a purse in his hip pocket. Then he grabbed the bottle of *viñ scully* by its base, smashed the neck off against the table's edge and let its contents flow down his throat. He rose to his full height, five feet two inches, bowed with a baleful smile that revealed a blindingly brilliant mouth and a garlicky breath, and walked out of the cheap *bistro,* the Alter Cockatoo, at soixante-quatre Arnold Cinq Boulevard in the Algerian quarter of Paris.

Shuddering, the KGB contact man, Vice-Consul Piotr Durak, swallowed his own Pernod as if to wash away the evil miasma he had felt in the man's presence.

"Do not expect LaBonza to answer you," the general had explained in his telephone conversation. "It is not for nothing that Torquemada LaBonza is known as 'The Silent One.' No one has ever heard his voice, except his victims. And they have all died in a bizarre manner, laughing insanely even as their life's blood ebbed from their torn bodies."

He recalled the rest of Bolshyeeyit's briefing. "We know very little about LaBonza, my dear Durak. We know that he is about thirty and was born out of wedlock to Maria Elena Smetana, a Basque gypsy, and Benvenuto LaBonza, an itinerant Corsican vaudevillian, in the back of a caravan wagon. His mother died at childbirth and he was raised by his father and a succession of paramours. The father, a chronic drunkard, eked out a beggarly living as a third-rate impressionist of American motion-picture stars in seedy theatres throughout Europe. He was killed in a knife fight when the boy was twelve, the rearing of the youth left to one Zorba the "Geek," a carnival performer. Thus the foundation for an embittered life was laid. As yet we neither know how he became an assassin nor why he does not speak. We do know of his work the last five years, the killing of the Yugoslavian *provocateur* Wsldz Ljmc by acid, the poisoning of the entire Katangan Board of Trade by curare mixed in their Junket, that curious death of the Frenchman, LeVoisin, who 'fell' off the freighter S.S. Tateleh in the Indian Ocean... many others. He has killed for the Union Corse, the Union Sicilone, the Union Teamstere and, most recently, for the Terrorist Union for Suppressing Hebrews."

"TUSH!" Durak had whispered, scarcely daring to speak the dreadful name.

"Yes, TUSH! He can be found usually at..." and here Bolshyeeyit had given Durak the name and location of the squalid cafe. "One thing more. He is easily recognized when he smiles. With his ill-gotten fees he not only had his rotting teeth replaced but also gilded his entire mouth structure. He is also known as 'The Man With the Golden Gums.'"

Filthy business, Durak said to himself. Thank heaven my duties for the fatherland rarely involve contacts with such amoral beasts. His connection made and the formidable Mrs. Durak safely accounted for at the beauty parlor, he decided he would spend a pleasant hour with a Mme. Denise Shtoomei, a curvaceous young circus acrobat at the Hotel Pierre DeSalinger, who, he knew from previous appointments, would, for a packet of francs, bend over backwards to please him.

"That's it, chums," said the jolly pilot. "Down there to your right. El Tiparillo."

Israel Bond, his forefinger idly dawdling inside the belly button of Anna, looked out of the window of the old sputtering B-17, flagship (in fact, the only ship) of Tailspin Tannenbaum's Flying Aardvark Airways. A solicitous sun sent a shaft through the mist, illuminating the mint-green Caribbean below. He checked his map; that guitarlike island to the left was Sal Salvador; to the North the odd land mass arranged in the general outline of a dollar sign, Costa Livin, and, yes, the cigar-shaped island Tannenbaum had pointed out—El Tiparillo!

"What is that golden stretch of land that cuts the island in two, Tailspin?"

"That's the famous no-man's land called The Band. Divides East El Tiparillo from West El Tiparillo. Or EET and WET as we call 'em for short."

Good man, this Tannenbaum, Bond thought. Knows his apples. He had spotted a few in Bond's lunch box, identified them rapidly. "That's a Delicious... those two are Macs... little bugger's a Winesap... the round orange thing's an orange."

Tannenbaum, Bond had learned during a pretakeoff chat, was one of those flying bums who once having had a taste of the wild blue yonder during the war could never again adjust to life on terra firma. He'd bought the shell-scarred B-17 from a war surplus warehouse at Key Luke on the tip of Florida, painted it a snazzy coral and pink and launched his one-man air service to the Caribbean. "Don't worry about this baby, Mr. Bond," he had chuckled between a continual crooning of "Comin' In On a Wing and a Prayer." "You're airborne with ol' Uncle Sam's No. 1 air ace. I shot down six Zeroes in the last big show."

"Six... that's a fair to middlin' number, Tailspin, but I've heard of guys who bagged twenty to twenty-five."

"From a Link Trainer?"

Bond had maintained a judicious silence from then on.

Besides Anna and himself, the only other travelers were his Israeli trio and an extremely tiny wild-eyed half-breed of some sort sporting a Dick Van Dyke beard and horn-rimmed glasses, whose spidery little body was clad in a tight-fitting pair of Jack-lemon slacks and matching suede sandals, set off by a leopardskin cocktail pull-over and a crimson beret with pompons. He did not seek conversation; seemed content to mutter from time to time and make notations on a pad.

Before Bond could ponder further on the unknown passenger, Tailspin cried: "Buckle up for safety, folks. We're coming in."

The next thing he knew he was roasting in midday tropical heat, his hand pumped vigorously by a moonfaced man in a Panama suit. "Shalom, Mr. Bond. I am Ben Bon Ami, Israel's consul on El Tiparillo. We will converse in my vehicle."

"Let's hold up on that until I drop the lady at a hotel. Can you recommend one?"

"One has been already arranged for you and your team. I was not expecting the lady."

"She is with me," Bond said. "Let me get her situated first."

Bon Ami, with great skill, guided his fire-engine-red fire engine through narrow, bump-filled streets replete with native markets, vendors selling tacos, the inevitable corner salesmen crying, *"Lotteria! Lotteria!* Win a million *marichals! Lotteria!"*

"Gambling is the passion here, my friend. These people will bet on anything," said Bon Ami, wiping cascades of sweat from his glistening temple. "Cockroach fights, the bulls, *jai alai,* beisbol, and so on. The men even bet on their sexual prowess."

"How interesting," said Anna, the first words she had spoken since landing. "What does the contest consist of?"

"It is perhaps too indelicate a subject for a lady's ears, *Señorita.* The concept of *Machismo,* virility... manhood, is uppermost in men's minds in these Latin islands. They flock to sexual betting parlors of Vera Hruba called 'los humpos' where... ah, but we have arrived." And Bon Ami seemed grateful for the interruption of his narrative.

The consul pulled into a driveway, chattered away in Spanish to a bespangled bell captain. "This is Bell Captain Belli. He will take the lady and her bags to a fine room in this estimable hotel which is the Nino Valdez. You gentlemen will join her later after we have our little talk. *Shalom, Señorita."*

"This, gentlemen," said Bon Ami, back in his office and very much the assured diplomat in his own surroundings, "is El Tiparillo." His pointer touched a dot on the wall map. "As you can see, we are in Vera Hruba, the capital city of West El Tiparillo, some 15 miles from The Band which, by agreement after the armistice in 1963, cuts this woeful isle in twain."

"Armistice?" asked Zvi.

"I was coming to that," said the consul.

Bond's ears, carefully tuned into the exposition he knew was coming, had caught something else. A buzzing. Circling around the overhead light set in a crystal chandelier was a wasp.

Bon Ami spotted it too. "One of the innumerable pests in these parts. Now, in 1962, leftist elements, Castroites, Muscovites and Pekingites, ceased their internal struggle for power long enough to call a temporary truce and unite behind a Russian puppet,

General Umberto D. Obratsov, who attempted to take over the
island from a foundering regime. The forces backing democracy
got behind a moderate, General Wesson y Oyl, and thus a bloody
civil war ensued. The United States backed Wesson y Oyl, sent
in money, arms, materiel, freedom fighters—guerrillas who
had been trained in leadership for this type of warfare at a
CIA-sponsored camp in Shaker Heights. All was going badly for
Wesson y Oyl when a sudden stroke of luck tipped the balance.
The CIA guerrillas were wiped out to a man in an ambush set up
by Peking's man here, that master of guile, Vi Teh Minh. Bereft
of this leadership, Wesson y Oyl found himself compelled to
wage his own battles, of which he won the next six, driving the
leftist coalition troops to their half of the island. Both sides were
vitiated by then and ready to call it a day. The UN negotiated
a settlement in which the island was halved; set up The Band
which its truce commission patrols. So at least half of the island
is run by a democratic form of government. Am I boring you, Oy
Oy Seven? I see your eyes are wandering elsewhere."

"Don't move, Bon Ami. Just keep perfectly still and do what
I tell you," said Bond in a low tense voice. He had seen the
loathsome thing crawl out of a crack in the adobe ceiling and
make its way to a spot about a foot over the consul's head.

It was a tarantula.

Black, hairy, big as a dinner plate.

Bond felt his body shaking. Only M. and the section
psychiatrist knew of his Melmacophobia, a fear of awakening in
the dead of night to find dinner plates crawling all over his body.

The wasp had seen it as well; zoomed near it.

"I think Dame Nature will resolve our problem," said Bond,
his hand clutching the front end of his wing-tipped Florsheim
cordovan, which he had planned to use to squash the huge
arachnid. "The wasp and the spider are mortal enemies."

But the combat never came. The wasp alighted next to the
tarantula. The two creatures undulated their feelers, actually
touched. As though it had received some message, the wasp
made a beeline for the open window and disappeared into a
hibiscus bush.

"Kill the goddam, filthy, ugly thing, Bond! Crush it... squash
it to smithereens!" It was little Nochum Spector, white as a
sheet done by new-improved Blue Cheer. He saw the quizzical
expression on Bond. "Damn it, you phony hero! Scared of a
spider? I'll kill the f— thing myself!" Nochum jumped on a

chair; swung his own shoe violently. It caught the lifted front legs which bared the fangs. The tarantula thrashed about in its death throes, fell with a plop into the corner of the room. "Kill it! Squash it!" screamed Spector again and lifted his pipe-cleaner of a leg to administer the quietus.

"Hold it!" Bond snapped. He pushed Spector away rudely; coldly watched the spider's ever-weaker struggles. Pulp oozed out of its side.

"Don't be so impetuous, Nochum," he said. "I do believe we should look at this first." He made a sudden pinching movement, wrested something from the top of the crushed tarantula.

Said Bond, scrutinizing a tiny disc about the size of a jellybean held between his forefinger and thumb, "I saw something on its back catch the light and gleam as it fell. This. What do you make of it, Itzhok? We can use that Technion know-how of yours right now."

Ben Franklin took the object, held it up to the light. A low whistle left his lips. "You won't believe this, gentlemen. It's a tiny transistorized listening device!"

"Geez, I'm sorry," Spector said. "I can't stand those damn hairy things. I wanted to crush it into a paste." Contrition was on his peach-whiskered baby face.

Bond did not comment on his apology. *"Gottenu!* On this damn island even the bugs are bugged!" And heard Zvi's appreciative bellow.

"An interesting problem and I wish we had time to delve into it further, Mr. Bond," said Bon Ami. "But you lads have been called in for a reason, a damn important one. Let us continue."

Bond lit a Raleigh; made an effort to push a few stray thoughts he'd been gathering out of his mind for the present. "Go on, Consul."

"Our country's problem is here." His hand fanned out on one side of the island. "This is WET, West El Tiparillo. This Star of David represents Israel's Peace Corps facility, Camp Kuchalein, which, as you see, is perilously perched on Mount Maidenhead, overlooking the jungle-covered Valley of the Blind. There is a famous motto coined by our own M. about this place. 'In the Valley of the Blind an optometrist shouldn't set up an office altogether.'"

"The old biddy's always coming up with crap like that," Nochum butted in.

Bon Ami ignored it. "The problem is this: We were asked to send a Peace Corps unit by General Wesson y Oyl because of the impressive record our people have made in Africa and Asia. For a while things went well. The natives, a poverty-stricken, superstitious lot, at first accepted us. We helped them grow food scientifically, tended to their sick, set up schools, cousin's clubs, dance studios, garment factories; in general, made our presence welcome on West El Tiparillo. Until a few weeks ago. Then scurrilous rumors began circulating throughout their villages that we were there to exploit them. An old native man who died of natural causes despite the efforts of our Dr. Marvin Browndorf was said to have succumbed to evil magic. Three of our volunteers were wounded by nocturnal snipers. Our potable water was spoiled by poison dumped into a well. Thank heaven, we had the foresight to put in an ample supply of seltzer. The worst happened two nights ago. A little boy was kidnapped from near his village; this note left behind. Read it, Bond."

It was a rough piece of parchment: "You will never see your Pablito again, Mr. and Mrs. Garcia. His blood will be offered to our pagan god as part of a Passover ritual. Be thankful that we of the Israeli Peace Corps have chosen his body to sacrifice on the altar."

Bond's chin pulled up belligerently. "Damn it! It's that vilest, basest of those pristine anti-Semitic canards! The lie that we must spill the blood of a non-Jewish child for Passover. Who's behind this, Bon Ami?"

The moonface shrugged its brows, "Anyone of the groups I mentioned—Peking, Moscow, Castro. They all have a deep interest in undermining us. We've shown the poor people of the *barrios* that progress can be made without the dear old hammer and sickle being shoved down their throats. Naturally, the Reds don't love us for that. Take a closer look at this map; you should become well acquainted with the terrain around Camp Kuchalein."

"What's this cross near the Peace Corps camp?" quizzed Itzhok.

"That's a convent, OLEO. Our Lady of the Eastern Order. Nice folks. They've been working unofficially with us on many projects. It's right on the top of the peak, if you'll notice. Halfway down is this point, cc, a summer colony for mediocre artists and musicians called Camp Camp. Weirdos. We don't bother with 'em too much. And here is the valley..." the pointer tip rested on a representation of a pagoda. "Stay the hell away from this place."

"Why?" said Bond.

"It's a bad place, the Temple of Hate. Run by a Chinaman named Dr. Nu. Quite unique, really. He operates a year-round resort for hate groups from all over the globe. 'Come here to hate at a special rate,' he advertises. All the pariahs pop up at his place: the Birchers, the KKK, Black Nationalists, some neo-Nazi groups from Deutschland."

"Our trouble could be coming from there, you know," Zvi said thoughtfully.

"Maybe. But until we know for sure stay away. Now, you boys will head out for Camp Kuchalein in the early bright. You can join a burro supply train that leaves from in front of the consulate at 5 A.M."

"Son-of-a-bitch!" Bond was in action again, hurling his cordovan at a black thing that skittered up through the crack and out of sight. "Another one of those creepy eavesdroppers! Bugged just like the spider. It was a roach this time, big bastard, about three inches long."

"Now hold on, Oy Oy Seven," said Bon Ami with annoyance. "They can't all be wired for sound."

"I'll bet my *tuchas* it was," said Bond. "Whoever is behind this now knows where we're going. I smell trouble."

Bon Ami smiled, a teacher patronizing an excited kindergarten pupil. "Maybe. But I want to talk to you alone for a minute, Bond. You'll excuse us, *boochereem?* See you tomorrow at 5."

Alone, Bon Ami turned to Bond, a serious shadow on the dark side of the moonface. "I have some bad news. This came for you." He pulled a large package from a closet. "It's from Lavi HaLavi. Came in this morning's pouch from Tel Aviv."

"What's the bad news?"

"HaLavi. He's gone off the deep end again."

"Oh, *Gottenu!* No!"

"Afraid so, Oy Oy Seven. According to a communication, he had just finished assembling this package for your personal use when he started to foam at the mouth. But here's the dispatch. Read it yourself."

"To Oy Oy Seven: Subject—Lavi HaLavi.

"At 8 P.M. yesterday the QM of M 33 and 1/3, who had just completed a number of combat devices, walked into M.'s office unannounced and began to berate her for not giving a laxative to an overstuffed chair in the corner. 'It is in pain,' he said. 'Badly needs a cleanout.' He then accused her of refusing to accept his 'brilliantly simple' plan for protecting our nation against any attack. It was, he said, the installation of a geodesic dome over the entire country with an elaborate air conditioning unit underneath. 'Not only will our land be safe from intruders, but we will never have another soccer game cancelled by rain.' At this point, M. pressed Alarm Aleph and three men in black hoods took him away to our branch's rest home, Foam Rubber Acres, in Galilee for treatment and a long period of seclusion.

"Yours truly, Dr. Hans Pippikel, section psychiatrist."

Bond's head rocked left-right-left-right with incredulity. Poor Lavi! Wacked out again. Easy to understand why. If I had to conceive the fantastic weapons and missions he does, I, too, would be bouncing around at Foam Rubber Acres every six months.

But Lavi had given the last ounce of his brain power on Bond's behalf. This was no time to wallow in pity. Whatever there was in this package was for use by a man licensed to kill.

"*Shalom*, Bon Ami. You'll be hearing from me." And he walked into the steaming street.

Heavy of heart, his mind troubled by the new developments, Israel Bond, HaLavi's package under his arm, trudged down Calle Cugat on his way to the Nino Valdez. I'm in for it now, he thought sardonically. Now I must tackle the whole damn Communist world, rescue a kidnapped child from God knows where or the Peace Corps will be subjected to a Latin blood bath, and ferret out a traitor. He'd had some thoughts about that last item during the consul's briefing. Nochum? "A phony hero" he called me. Does he hate me that much? How anxious he was to mash the spider! And that crack about M., his own aunt, "an old biddy." Is all this enough to pin the tail on the donkey? Then there was Anna, lovely, wanton, constantly inflaming his every red corpuscle. Could she really be trusted? And, if so, what's in the cards for her and me? Marriage? But I have sworn to my late sainted mother to stand under the traditional wedding canopy with a daughter of Zion. Would Anna convert? And is the Paradise Wedding Hall in the Bronx all booked up?

This whole damn thing sounds like a teaser for next week's *Peyton Place*, he told himself. Back to work, Oy Oy Seven.

At the intersection of Calle Desi-Lu and Cinco de Virginia Mayo he saw a boisterous crowd pushing its way into a large, obviously new, building. A neon sign flashed on and off: "FREEZERIA."

Bond quickly realized what the place was. Freezerias—the mushrooming slumber palaces in which reposed the recently dear departed.

The concept of freezing the dead, until that glorious day when an ever-improving medical science could discover the curse for the various maladies that had shuffled them off this mortal coil, then unfreeze and cure them, was spreading all over the world. He had once read an article on the subject which listed a price range of $8,000 to $50,000 for the cost of freezing your dear Uncle Seymour a few hours after clinical death. It was like anything else in life, he imagined. You get what you pay for. For eight grand, he reckoned, the best you could expect would be to have Uncle Seymour thrown in with the Sara Lee cheesecakes at the local A & P. But for fifty big ones... ah, then you got the individual freezer with fresh flowers placed on the chest everyday, the weekend outings by a family come to see that all was well ("Mummy, he's smiling".... "Why not, precious? He's just sleeping until the big Reveille Day, that's all"... "Gee, you know, Syl, I think he actually gained weight. The old boy looks good"), the plug guard (for that kind of money surely one was entitled to have a man guard the plug; who could tell when some enemy who owed Seymour a bundle would yank it and leave Uncle to rot?) and the emergency generator in case of power failure. And, Bond surmised, today's four-letter obscenities would have no sting at all in fifty years. The truly shocking four-letter words of future generations would be "melt" and "thaw." And the most despicable epithets—"mother-melter," "father-thawer."

Death. It's on my mind. Why? asked Bond of himself. There was an answer from his inner voice: Because this lousy island smells of death.

The smell of death was in Anna's nostrils, though she did not recognize it as such. It encroached slowly upon the scented bath powder she had used to sweeten her body in preparation for another lunar field trip with this darkly handsome Israeli of hers. While dusting the peaks of her fine breasts, she became aware of it. Garlic. The odor of garlic.

Then she saw the grinning golden mouth in the mirror. Just as she was about to scream, she heard the voice: "You are going to die, my lovely one." And even though terror-stricken, she began to laugh, irrepressible peal after peal.

The hand squeezed the trigger twice. Anna, still howling at the top of her lungs, fell dying, blood spurting from her stomach on the plush Gulistan Saroyan carpet. The door opened, startling the little man in the gypsy garb, who pushed through the drapes and bolted down the fire escape.

"B & T time again," a cheery Bond called; then froze in horror.

She was still laughing when he found her. "Golden gums... that voice... golden gums... hee hee ha ha...." And she died in his arms.

10
"Ah Got De Blues"

"From all you have told me," said Bon Ami, with honest sympathy, "it adds up to Torquemada LaBonza. The eerie death laugh, her dying reference to 'golden gums.' Yes, it was LaBonza the 'Silent One,' the 'Man with the Golden Gums.'" And he proceeded to fill Bond in on every scrap of information in his file relating to the infamous slaughterer. "I think you've had it on this assignment, Oy Oy Seven. I'll wire M. for another Double-Oy immediately."

"No. I'm seeing this one through... for Anna," said Bond. He sat on the consul's terrace looking at the million and one lights of Vera Hruba. "She got what was intended for me. This is KGB revenge all the way; I can sense it." He crushed his fragile wineglass in his hand, not feeling or caring about the wetness trickling out of his palm's lifeline.

"Please allow me to take care of the final arrangements for Anna."

"Thanks, Bon Ami. And please, put this in the coffin with her. It's my picture. She would have wanted it. Wait," he said, his voice cracking. "Let me write a little something on it."

"Of course."

He scribbled, "To Anna, sincere best wishes, Israel Bond." Then to his host: "I loved her, you know." And he pressed his bloodied hand in Bon Ami's and walked out into the indifferent night.

Ill-tempered, loaded-down burros braying, the supply train wended its way at a crawl through the green hell of the West El Tiparillan jungle. Snow-capped Mount Maidenhead lay six leagues and three chukkers away. Already their clothes were drenched with sweat powerful enough to turn their nylon-fibre garb back into coal, water, and air.

"Must be one hundred and thirty in the shade, for God's sake," grunted Zvi.

"It's one hundred and thirty-five in the shade, to be exact," responded the precise Itzhok Ben Franklin, consulting his thermometer.

"*Gottenu!*" exclaimed Bond. "I'm afraid to even guess what it is here in the sun."

"Ninety-six."

He slapped at a botfly trying to bore into his neck. "These damn burros are slow as hell. Can't they go any faster?"

"I doubt it," Zvi said. "They're carrying one hundred sacks of matzoh meal, two hundred pounds to a sack."

"What the hell for?" Bond fired back.

"The Peace Corps plans to throw a gigantic Passover Seder meal for the poor in a couple of nights."

"*If* there's a Peace Corps, you mean. We still have to find little Pablito."

Good lads! he thought. They, of course, knew all about Anna and were trying to make light conversation to take his mind off the awful night. Except Nochum, that little snotnose, who rode ahead, his face an insolent mask.

When the sting pierced his right shoulder he first thought some giant jungle bee had dive-bombed him. Then he saw the puff of smoke and heard Nochum's anguished cry: "Ambush!"

Down dove Bond, flattening his body in the rotting vegetation. "Take cover!" Then there was a sound that set his adrenal glands flowing in terror. The sound of a miniature sort of thunder... and the pounding, earth-shaking sound of a stampede. He knew what it meant.

Buffalo leeches!

The filthy bloodsuckers were on him now, drinking deeply of his claret which poured out of three dozen punctures from ankle to thigh. *Gottenu!* don't let them go higher!

The sound of their munching was drowned out by a sudden horrible scream that trailed off. Nochum! And yells through the green, impenetrable rain-forest walls. "You meet your maker, Israeli dogs! We cut out your tongues, Jews!" Now a strident falsetto: "Marine, tonight you die! Marine, tonight you die!"

An ex-Jap *soldat*, no doubt, fighting the wrong war, he mused, but no less malevolent. *"Banzai gezunt,* Tojo!" he screamed in rebuttal.

"Bond! Over here. I'm hit!" Zvi! His hands frantically trying to cover a dark stain spreading over his shirt front.

"How bad?" said Bond, manfully ignoring his own shoulder wound and the gnawing below.

"Chest. *Oy vay,* it hurts! I was trying to reach poor Nochum. He's had it."

"How?"

"I rode..." Zvi coughed... "up to him when the first shot went off. It's awful, Bond, awful! He's lying face down in a pit... must be a hundred spikes through him."

Bond lit a Raleigh, pressed it to Zvi's blood-flecked mouth. "Poison, too, I'll wager. This must be Vi Teh Minh and his China boys. It's their kind of show. They're jungle fighters, you know."

Zvi inhaled. Thwack! He pitched forward. Now there was a second stain between his shoulder blades. "The last little joke for an old pal, Oy Oy Seven..."

Bond gulped, fighting back scalding tears. "Well, Zvi," he grinned weakly. "You got it in the chest... you got it in the back... and with all that you still haven't had a bellyful."

"Oh, *mommeleh*... I haven't got a bellyful. What a f— mind on that bastard! Oh, *mommeleh*..." his laugh and life gurgled out. Lovable Zvi Gates was dead.

The scum! The f— scum! "All right, you dirty yellow slant-eyed bastards! Uh, no racial derogation intended, fellows." He tore at a ring on his belt. "Let's see how you like a pineapple in your Chink faces." He stood up, cocked his arm, let the pineapple fly square in the face of an oncoming guerrilla. Its spines drilled into his eyes; the rotten insides squirted into the man's mouth. The marauder gagged and ran off vomiting. Good! But at least you'll live, you bastard! It's just a goddam shame it wasn't a grenade, Bond thought.

Wait! HaLavi's package! He raced back to his burro and cut the bundle loose with a slash of his machete. Tearing away the paper, he pulled out a half-dozen jars containing bright red gelatinous matter. "Mother Margolies' Old World Boysenberry Jelly," the labels read.

He tucked the jars into his coat jacket and slid on his belly through the brush, a Jewish fer-de-landsman bent on revenge. Five of them! Grouped about a mortar, one of them about to pump in a shell. "Here, you bastards! Let's have a jam session!" He hurled all six of the jars into the Vi Teh Minh quintet. They went off simultaneously, merging into one red ball of flame. He heard their screams, smelled barbecuing flesh.

"It must be napalm jelly... 'cause jam don't shake like that!" he shouted.

"Bond, over here!" Itzhok now! Was he cashing in his chips as well?

"You all right, kid?"

"I think so. Something's got my foot."

Bond leaned over. "It's a Malay snare. Got your ankle. Don't move. There may be poison on the thorns." He cut it away but, as he did, he noticed Itzhok's face was already bluish in pallor. He slit the *Sabra's* trouser leg, saw a telltale pinprick of a hole near the calf.

"I feel numb, Oy Oy Seven."

"Hold on! Hold on!" He finished cutting off the thornstudded vine. But Itzhok was not answering. And never would again.

I've lost all three... in one swell foop. My gutsy little team is gone. I'm alone in a scorching emerald wilderness, with no men and four dozen stinking burros carrying twenty thousand pounds of matzoh meal. He began to laugh wildly. Any second now he expected a bullet between the eyes. But aside from the hum of insects and the jabbering of howler monkeys, the jungle was silent. Looks like my jelly broke up the traffic jam, he thought. Zvi, would that you could have heard that one, old comrade.

He was starting to feel the loss of blood; heat, hum and howl combined with the moldy odor of the jungle to set his head spinning. He fell into the muck.

Pain! Something sticking in his shoulder.

"Look, angel," he croaked. "I know you have to fasten on my wings, but for God's sake—you should pardon the expression—use Scotch tape. That f— safety pin is killing me."

The figure in white looming above him said, "He's coming out of it, Sister. More sulfa, please."

Bond opened a cautious eye. His angel was a bulky man with warm brown eyes. In a white smock. A doctor! "Who are you?"

"Ben Kildare I ain't. My handle's Marv Browndorf, doctor attached to the ill-fated Peace Corps camp. This lady is Sister Kate. And no shimmy jokes about her. She's heard 'em all."

"Ill-fated?"

"Yes, a column of them hit the camp at the same time the advance guard ambushed you. We heard the noise and came down."

"Where am I?" He reached for a Raleigh.

"You're in a bed at the convent OLEO. They very kindly gave our remaining corpsmen refuge. We've only got six left out of twenty. You, I'm afraid, have none left."

"I know," Bond said. "I saw two of my boys get it. And Spector?"

"There was no time to pull him out of the pit. Besides, there are a couple tons of scavenger ants cleaning up down there. And we had to get you up here fast. Wounds fester like mad here in the tropics. By the way, the monks got your burro train up here. The matzoh's piled up in a nice cool cellar, so don't worry about it."

"That's the least of my worries. But what the hell are monks doing in a convent?"

Dr. Browndorf probed his Johnson & Humphrey Q-tip again into the wound, causing Bond to cry out. "Go ahead. Yell all you want. What are monks doing here? Well, there are some heavy chores around here the sisters can't handle. Besides, these monks are in their sixties. Nice old coots, Brother Thelonius and Brother Julius. I like 'em."

Bond pulled himself up. "Those goddam buffalo leeches...." He looked at his legs, dotted with minute scars.

"Used an old Burmese trick to get rid of 'em. Touched 'em with a lighted cigarette and they fell off. Funny thing, though, I used one of your cigarettes on a single leech and the rest of 'em fell off, curled up and died without even being touched. What do you smoke, anyway?"

"Look, Doc, I've got to get the hell out of here. That kidnapped kid must be found or Israel's name will be mud in El Tiparillo and all of Latin America."

Dr. Browndorf frowned. "You nuts? You've lost blood and you're weak as a kitten. It's beddy-bye for you, Bond."

"Like hell!" and he inched up painfully. "See, I'm standing. Now, get me a horse. I want to nose around this area and there isn't much time."

"It's your funeral," the doctor shrugged. "But good *mahzel* and good hunting, Oy Oy Seven!"

In no hurry at all, and not about to be pushed, was scraggly Old Kemtone, the bag of bones and alleged horse he had borrowed from the considerate monks.

Deliberately it picked its way down the rocky trail to the valley, stopping now and then to nibble the fragrant top of a locoweed bush, whinnying as it chomped the stuff down.

"Well, here I am... on my high horse," he sallied. "Come on, you glorified dachshund. Speed it up."

Old Kemtone answered by rearing up. Bond felt himself flying backwards. Splash! He was up to his neck in a brass monkey-cold mountain stream, ears rocked by the strident love-calls of the brass monkeys.

As he stood shivering he heard a voice through the roar of the torrent. A sweet and low voice, crooning a soulful old blues song:

> *"Ah got de blues; oh Lawd, Ah got de blues,*
> *Ah said Ah got de blues; oh Lawd, Ah got de blues,*
> *Oh yeah, Ah got de blues; oh, Lawd, Ah got de blues."*

He recognized it in a second. It was one of the great blues torchants of jazz history, titled "Guess What Ah Got?" And that voice? So familiar! Didn't he have a recording of that voice doing that very ditty? Of course!

As he tried to squeeze the information from his fogged mind, he saw near a tree two sensationally formed brown legs, just an enticing flash of thigh... and then he heard a deep growl. There was something tawny and spotted moving out to the end of the tree limb.

Tigre! A powerful jaguar, undisputed king of Latin-American jungles. He heard a tiny frightened "oh" behind the tree. The blues singer was quite aware of the deadly stalker above her, crouched to spring.

Bond waded hip-deep into the frigid waters, unarmed; yet prepared to take the brunt of the snarling cat's lunge. Damn fool! I left HaLavi's new rifle in Old Kemtone's stirrup.

Three hundred yards away was another rifle at the ready, an angry eye pressed against the telescopic lens, the back of Israel Bond's head split neatly in the T-sight. A cheap Delicado cigarette dangled from the lips of Torquemada LaBonza.

He squeezed the trigger just as the *tigre* roared and zeroed in on Bond. The Israeli bent as the cat's paws ripped his shoulders, the foul breath from the decayed flesh in its teeth nearly causing him to pass out.

It was the brow of the *tigre* that was stove in by the soft-nosed bullet from the barrel of the high-powered Tanaka rifle. *El tigre* sank, was borne away by the rushing stream.

"*Merde!*"* groaned LaBonza. His target was now behind the tree, out of range. He climbed back on his rented quarter horse, slipped another quarter into the metered coin box strapped to its neck and rode off. He would bide his time. Another opportunity would come.

"You can come out now, my dear," Bond said. His shoulders ached terribly. The cat's claws had torn into each one. Luckily the epaulets on his Ramar of the Jungle pukkah-sahib jacket had been thick enough to absorb most of the gouging. But he knew from the hot streamlets rolling down each shoulder that *el tigre* had left a partial souvenir.

"One moment more, please." A sweet, well-modulated voice from the other side of the thick foliage. "Well, here I am, sir, and my heartfelt thanks for your selfless act of heroism in saving my unworthy life. My daily bath is rarely interrupted in such a dramatic manner."

Heavenly, utterly heavenly was the face that emerged from behind the tree, that of the most gorgeous Negro girl Israel Bond had ever seen. Two gentian-violet eyes in a finely chiseled setting, chin, nose, lips of classical proportions. All this he noticed moments later. It was her clothes that stunned the exhausted, panting secret agent. His new fascinating companion of the El Tiparillan rain forest was a nun!

---

*   "Bad show!"

11
Poems To Touch The Heart, Turn The Stomach

Now Bond's memory came through for him.

"That face, that voice, that song. I remember now. Sid Mark Jazz Disc 190009-V, my most prized waxing. You are the former Sweetcakes Simmons, the world's top jazz *chanteuse,* who deserted the smoky niteries of Manhattan a few years ago to take the vows."

"Yes," she smiled. "Your memory serves you well and it is flattering to be remembered with such warmth. I am that woman, now known as Sister Sweetcakes... more popularly by the public as the Swinging Nun."

"The Swinging Nun!" He could not keep the admiration out of his reply. "Truly, Sister, you have not lost one whit of that puristic sultriness that made you the undisputed queen of the blues. Why did you give it up for this Godforsaken island?"

"You have answered your own query, sir. You said 'Godforsaken.' That is precisely why I am here. There is a burning need for the Lord of Hosts on El Tiparillo. But come. We shall talk as we return to OLEO. You, of course, will be my guest for dinner."

He suddenly lurched, fell forward, his body snagged in the tree.

"Oh, but you are hurt badly. I see blood on your shoulders."

He did not answer. For the second time in as many hours Israel Bond was unconscious.

"Wiseguy, Mr. Supersecret Agent Know-It-All. How damn long can you go on abusing that mighty body of yours?" It was Dr. Browndorf again, hopping mad, yet unmistakable pity showing on his face.... Sister Sweetcakes, her cool fingers on his fevered brow.

"This man is a secret agent, Doctor?"

"Yes, Sister. He is Israel Bond of Eretz Israel. Don't let that boyish look delude you. He kills for a living."

"Oh, dear!" the nun looked horrified. "Such a fine-looking man and so well-spoken. I find that hard to believe."

"It is true. Look after him, Sister, for a while. I must treat our six Peace Corps survivors."

"Then your camp is finished."

"Yes, overrun, burnt to the ground. Perhaps by the same people who snatched poor little Pablito and spread that filthy rumor about the Passover bloodletting."

"Do not worry, Doctor. I shall tend to him."

Bond moaned. "Brandy, Sister Sweetcakes... served in a decanter of Ezra Stoneware at a room temperature of 73.1 degrees."

"There is none, I fear," she said. "But the good brothers do have some homemade wine." She held a goblet to his lips. It was a bitter brew, aged the old Lombardy way, in deep dirty ashtrays. "If you are hungry there is some food, simple, but nourishing. Cheese and bread."

"Monks' Bread, 111 lay you ten to one," he jested, the sight of this amazing woman reviving his zest for life.

"As a matter of fact, it is," she laughed charmingly.

"I can't figure you out, Sister. Beauty, poise, sensitivity. And yet you bury your loveliness in a cowl and habit. Why?"

She pressed a Raleigh into his swollen lips, scratched a match on the heel of her thick black shoe. "It is a dreary story, Mr. Bond. I was at the height of a dazzling career, appearances in the smartest supper clubs, records selling phenomenally, the quarry of rich men of all races pressing diamonds and chinchillas upon me.... I drank too much; indulged in meaningless affairs with men I did not love. A life without purpose or form. I awoke mornings with the taste of dissolution in my mouth."

"I myself have found that Listerine—"

"Then," she went on, not noticing his helpful interjection, "I met a wonderful man, Cardinal Musial, a prince of the Church, who convinced me that my life could yet have meaning. I became a nun, forsook my empty, glittering, twelve o'clocktail lush life. I have found serenity and hope here at OLEO. Would that my tormented half-brother could find the same."

"Your half-brother?"

"Yes, Beaster Simmons, a man of rare insight and creative genius, who, alas, has been psychologically warped by his hatred of white people. He has changed his name to Baldroi LeFagel and is a leading poet and playwright of the so-called angry school."

"Yes," said Bond. "I seem to recall one of his novels. I have it in a paperback. I found it soul-searing, unsettling. For a moment I was ashamed of being a Caucasian. However, I did purchase a Moms Mabley album. And I took out a subscription to *Muhammud Speaks.*"

"What a coincidence!" she brightened. "Baldroi is its night club editor. As a matter of fact, he is—"

"He is here."

There in the doorway was the little bearded man Bond had seen on Tannenbaum's plane. The secret agent's orbs bulged in disbelief. Baldroi LeFagel stood posed like a ballerina, a toe pointed daintily at Bond. He wore an attractive, white Courrèges middy blouse and skirt, with black buttons and piping. His little feet were jammed in that fashion-setter's famed boots. He pirouetted over to Bond's bedside and flicked his hand across Bond's face in contempt. Sister Sweetcakes gasped. He paid her no mind, began to recite:

> *"You negate my existence, Mistuh Charlie Whitey Man,*
> *You have held me in chains since the world began.*
> *You have bruised my flesh and, worse, my psyche,*
> *Let me tell you, Whitey, yo' black slave no likey!*
> *From out of the ghettos there comes the roar,*
> *Of a new black man who knows the score.*
> *We will seethe in your streets, sound trumpet and*
>   *drum,*
> *I promise you, Whitey, we shall overcome!*
> *And now you're frightened, Mr. Charlie White 'fay,*
> *Of our new-found strength which burgeons each day,*
> *Yes, now you wanna make up for yo' chains 'n' dogs 'n'*
>   *whips,*
> *I'll make up, yes, on my terms—kiss me on the lips!"*

"Baldroi!" Her voice scourged him. "Mr. Bond is wounded and burning with fever. And he is my guest. Let him be!"

"One sweet kiss?" whimpered LeFagel.

"Begone! You shame me!"

With a wink and "see you later, Whitey, sweetie," the poet exited.

Oy Oy Seven lifted himself. "I must find the boy, Sister. And you must help me."

"Please lie down, Mr. Bond. You must rest."

LeFagel popped back. "Here's my latest, you adorable bitch," and he darted his tongue at Bond. "Dig this, sweet pappy:

> *"I have a pet cobra named Alger,*
> *On his sweet fangs I give him a kiss,*
> *When I tell him 'bout them bad white folks,*
> *You should hear Alger hiss!"*

The telephone at his bedside erupted. "It's for you, Sister Sweetcakes," Bond said. "Long distance from New York. Somebody named Marty O'Marty from Rock of Ages Records."

"Ah," she smiled. Was there the tiniest trace of longing for the old days in her violet eyes? "Dear Marty. He was my agent and now owns the record company that keeps after me to record a religious album. I may yet yield, Mr. Bond. Our parish here is quite low on funds and Cardinal Musial has given me permission to do it—if it is done tastefully and reverently. It might amuse you to listen in, Mr. Bond."

She placed that divine head next to his and for a moment Bond forgot her sacred calling. What a woman! He could fall in love with a sublime creature like this in twenty seconds. And easily be faithful to her twice as long. Already the memory of Anna, that slattern, was beginning to fade.

"Hiyah, Sister!" The high-pressure voice of a real New York "go-getter."

"Hello, dear Marty."

"Look, Sister. We ain't had a hit album on the charts for two years. Whadda yuh say yuh break down and cut one for good old Rock of Ages, huh? Something with class, naturally, but with an appeal to the wonderful kids who are the principal record buyers in today's market."

"Well, Marty, I—"

"Great! You'll do it! Actually you don't have to pray *that much,* do you? I mean, uh, well, couldn't you maybe cut one o' them lesser masses? I mean, what the hell— uh, no offense, Sister, I'm a good Cat'lic meself... well, you should hear the tunes that me and my A&R man picked out for the date. Dig these, Sister. 'Forget the Baubles 'n' Bangles—Just Give Me the Beads'... that's class... 'I Love Parish'; we kinda rewrote one of them Cole Porter things. He can't sue us now anyway. 'Paul or Nothing At all,' 'I Married an Angel,' 'Nun Domenticar'... somethin' Eyetalian always adds that *distingué laplume de ma tante,* if yuh know what I mean.... 'There's No Place Like Rome,' that's like for the family crowd... old folks buy records, too; I don't knock 'em, believe me.... 'It's Gettin' To Be A Habit with Me'—there's a grabber, a pun 'n' cuter than hell... again, no offense, Sister; I personally got three kids enrolled in the CYO... and we'll send down our hot new group, A Man Called Peter and the Padres, for backgrounds; they'll do the oo-wahs under the melody... plus technicians, equipment... you got a real jungle down there, ain't you, Sister? With birds and monkeys and all that? Maybe like we could even work in some of them in the background with the oo-wahs and rang-a-langs, like the Martin Denny sound, huh? And dig the title of the album: 'I Love Him, Yea, Yea, Yea!' The album cover has you in the nun suit, except you're in a Rolling Stones' wig, see? With a look of reverence on your sweet face, of course; don't get me wrong. So it's all set. The whole bunch, singers, sound men, will be down there in a chartered plane in a day. Uh, if you can spare a moment from divine contemplation... and, God knows, that's important... I ain't knockin' it... uh, maybe you could like rehearse some of the jungle birds and beasties. They'll get union scale, of course. Or we'll donate to any charity dear to your wonderful heart. I'm personally gonna direct this session myself, Sister. Maybe we can get a photo spread outa *True Magazine.* Or maybe even Jim Bishop could come down and write a human interest thing: 'Nun Swings, So Little Children May Walk.' Nice tide, huh? It's got heart. I'll throw to Jimmy; he might dig it. Anyhow it don't hurt to have a Bishop on our side, does it, Sister? Ha! Ha! Little inside joke there. See you soon. Don't take any wooden idols!"

Sister put down the phone, quite dazed. "He's a hard man to say no to, Mr. Bond."

"Wonder if he's interested in a group called the Rocking Rabbis? Or four Anglican caretakers... the Beadles?"

"You have a unique sense of humor, Mr. Bond," the nun observed.

"It's you, Sister. You bring out the best in me. But now to business. I've got to find that child. Any leads for me?"

"Yes. One. The last time he was seen he was playing in the vicinity of that godless place, the Temple of Hate."

"Then that's where I'm going tonight."

"No!" she cried. "In your condition? And even if you were healthy, you can't go wandering about this unfamiliar jungle at night."

"Perhaps," Bond suggested, "you would guide me there. I'd be glad of the company, Sister, especially yours."

Her eyes grew soft. "I can't let you stumble in there alone. Meet me in front of OLEO after evening vespers."

He pressed her hand; then on an impulse lifted it to his lips.

"You mustn't..." she said in a tiny voice.

"Tonight then. The Temple of Hate... and Dr. Nu."

12
A Good Skate

A far more tractable beast under the familiar guidance of the nun, Old Kemtone clopped his cantrece nylon hooves at a leisurely clip, Bond and Sister Sweetcakes wedged in the deep trough of his swayed back. So emaciated was the horse that Bond thought he was sitting upon a xylophone and indeed, by certain posterior movements he was able to play "I'm Walking Behind." Both he and Sister were silent, though they felt the mysterious beginnings of a subtle electricity between them. This incandescent creature, his heart told him, was the supreme example of womanhood. Could Corporal Annatevkah at her best ever have matched this magnificent specimen of physicality and soul? He felt in his shirt pocket for the garnet ring he had very sensibly taken from Anna's dying hand. Life and love must go on, Bond, he told himself, and one doesn't splurge on nearly a tenth of a carat every day.

Halfway down to the Valley of the Blind, the strains of a familiar operetta filtered through the liana vines and odiferous *johni-johni* trees.

"It is from Camp Camp," she informed him. "Each night the artists and musicians put on some kind of a production for their guests. Usually, they take some well-known musical work and augment it with highly modern touches."

Bond's powerful field glasses were trained on an open air stage. "I know the music. I see a mezzo-soprano singing an aria from Oscar Straus' *The Chocolate Soldier.*"

"'My Hero,' I believe," Sister added.

"Correct. 'My Hero' it is. Only she is singing it to a gigantic Italian sandwich cradled in her arms."

They heard the cries of the audience exhorting the singer on to new artistic heights: "Let's go, mezzo! Let's go, mezzo!"

"From this point on it can be dangerous, Mr. Bond," she said. "There are many guards in the vicinity of the temple."

I won't worry, he thought. HaLavi's new rifle looks to have the firepower of a whole regiment. It was strapped to the horse's side, 75 Melba rounds in the magazine. Bond glanced at its unusual stock, four times wider than any he'd ever handled. He knew why and grinned. That HaLavi genius!

I could use that genius tonight, he conceded. This mystery and my problems are mushrooming by the minute. Where is the boy? Which of the three dead Israelis had masqueraded as Rotten Roger Colfax, the traitor? Or was Roger none of them at all? Who is this Dr. Nu and why has he chosen to make money out of the bigotry in this world? That shot that killed *el tigre*... was it fired by LaBonza? And Sister Sweetcakes... does she know what I feel for her? Could she give up this ennobling but barren way of life and take my hand forever? Will the cost of the Annatevkah woman's funeral be deducted unfairly from my salary?

"We are here," the nun whispered.

"Stay here with this noble steed. Or better still, Sister, get thee to thy nunnery. It's my show from here on in."

"May God go with you, Israel Bond."

"See you in church, Sister. Mine, I hope."

Pushing two branches aside, he got his first glimpse of the Temple of Hate bathed in the whiteness of a full moon that imparted a chalky patina to its gangrenous green-grey walls.

It was approximately two hundred feet tall, he estimated, with Byzantine-style minarets standing like spears at each of its four corners. From a number of windows light blazed and drunken voices sang cursed and shouted. The hate set is having a wingding tonight, he thought. Pretty soon they'll be swapping all the "Jew-boys" jokes: "Hey, Abie, vash der toilet paper; der landlord says ve got to move." Yes, Bond, you try to push the brotherhood bit all your life, go out of your way to fit in, but you meet rejection wherever you go. But what else can you expect from *goyim?*

Drop the philosophy of alienation bit, Oy Oy Seven; there's a job to be done.

He tied handkerchiefs over his shoes to muffle his footsteps and walked into a large paved area between the edge of the jungle and the temple. For cars? No, there were none around. A place to land a helicopter, more likely. As if to confirm his suspicion, he heard the chopper far off and flattened his body in the shadows cast by the pillars of the main entrance.

It came down a minute later. Out stepped a short man in a sporty Tyrolean-type Adams hat with a sprig of edelweiss stuck into the brim and a black trenchcoat, his face hidden by its pulled-up collar. Two Orientals in ski-type outfits, rifles slung over their shoulders, walked out of the doorway to greet him. Then up went the chopper in a swift vertical climb.

Whoever the visitor was he seemed to be accorded the highest respect. Bond could make out the guards' voices now.

"A pleasure to see you back, Rotten Roger, sir. Dr. Nu has been anxiously awaiting you. You'll be pleased to know that the Russian courier dropped off the million rubles today."

Rotten Roger Colfax! So there he was. And obviously not one of my poor dead lads, thank heaven!

The trio walked into the temple but, just before the door slammed thunderously, he heard a fragment of a sentence. "... greatest terror organization the world has ever known" and something that sounded like "Spector."

Spector? Were they making some callous jibe about little Nochum's agonizing end in the stake-lined pit? Wait a second, Bond. "Greatest terror organization the world has ever known." Could it be true? Yes, you dunce. There are *two* words pronounced like Nochum's surname and one of them is spelled— SPECTRE! Then the fabled organization of infinite evil was a reality! Naturally, it would have been the diabolical agency behind Pablito's kidnapping, the attack on the Israeli camp, the murders of Zvi, Itzhok and Nochum. Paid handsomely for these foul services by the Russians (he had already heard of one Russki payoff) and probably behind every significant act of terrorism and revolution on this benighted island. No doubt the Chinese and Fidelistas were kicking into the SPECTRE treasury, too. It made sense. If anything ever went awry there would be no proof of their involvement in these heinous undertakings.

If he had not been so engrossed in unraveling the puzzle, he would have seen the six-inch isosceles scorpion coming down the door, springing onto his neck and—arrgh!—its venomous sting flaying his wounded shoulder. He brushed it off with a shiver, ground his heel into it until it was a mashed heap of protein. Except for the diamond-hard black disc in the middle of the mess. Another transistor 'bug'! They know I'm here; *Katz* is out of the bag!

An alarm sounded in the temple, sending a bevy of uniformed Orientals vaulting out with brandished carbines. Shots echoed through the night, one of them kicking up a chunk of cement and hurling it into his face, opening a gash on his cheek. He kneeled, aimed HaLavi's rifle.

Zetz! Zetz! Zetz! The Moishe Dyan model spoke its message three times; that many guards fell screaming. Good! Now three from Column B! But more were swarming out as the alarm went off again. He saw a flash, felt a hot projectile skin his ankle. There were two dozen of them now, lined up between Bond and the edge of the paved strip. Beyond it lay the safety of the thick jungle. How to get past them? No time to stop and pick them off. Too many!

Israel Bond's brain clicked out a solution in a microsecond. His finger jabbed at a button in the huge rifle stock. Four wheels slid out of the wood and Bond was now standing atop a skateboard!

He crouched low over it, pushed his toe into the cement, kicked out to pick up momentum and smashed through the first line of guards. He felt nails futilely tearing at his face as he bowled them over. Now he was ramming into the second line, the Dyan firing automatically, ripping ankle bones and insteps, as the skateboard sped on.

A few feet more and freedom! But at the jungle's edge he saw a figure slip out from behind a *yeki-yeki* bush. It kneeled in the classic rifleman's position, bent a finger.

Bond ducked. In time to save his life; too late to avoid being hit altogether. Torquemada LaBonza's Tanaka sang its *saki! saki!* One slug creased the dark, cruelly handsome forehead and Bond went down face first in the cement.

The last thing he remembered, before a blessed Ken Murray blackout, was lying on the airstrip looking blearily at a pair of elegant brocaded Chinese sandals with curled-up toes.

And a mocking voice: "Welcome to the Temple of Hate, Mr. Israel Bond. My leader and I have been expecting you. I am Dr. Nu."

13
Herbie

"I shall give you a capsulized history of my illustrious life, Mr. Bond," said the cool articulate voice of Dr. Nu to the bound Bond, who sat in a chair, blood dripping from his shoulder, ankle, and head into a pool on the floor, a feast for a herd of buffalo leeches and a vampire bat on a silken tether, the other end tied about the Chinaman's right hand. "Drink sparingly of this rich Jewish blood, my beloved bat, Masterson," the doctor said fondly to his pet. "Too much and you'll get diabetes."

"I don't think I'm particularly interested in your life," Oy Oy Seven said with a stiffness that matched that of his ripped aching body. "So get on with whatever you've dreamed up for me."

"Not interested, Mr. Bond?" Dr. Nu's rebuke was mild, which made it all the more menacing. "Topjob, put our celebrated guest in the proper frame of mind for history."

Gottenu! A bludgeon split the side of his cheek, reopening the wound. It was the calloused side of a hand swung by a stocky Asiatic in a loose-fitting white robe.

"Meet my personal bodyguard. Topjob, so named because his favorite libation is an American liquid detergent of some potency. Like myself he is half-Chinese, born in Korea, and extremely adept at karate. He holds a black belt. Everyday he practices for an hour, chopping those awesome hands into Del Monte's creamed corn."

"How in hell can they get so callused from hitting creamed corn?"

"It is still in the can. Excellent work, Topjob. As a reward you may eat the leeches and Masterson. *Sayonara*, old bat."

Bond took his first good look at Dr. Nu. He was an unbelievable caricature of a man, bigger than life; from the tip of his curled-up toes to the green velvet Mitsubishi hat he must have easily stood six feet six inches. His face jarred Bond. Only one of the eyes was slanted. And his hair was a most un-Oriental ash blond. The bean pole body was clad in a dazzling long coat of Cantonese silk and black pajamas. On the coat were superb Hakusai water colors of great moments in Far Eastern history; Genghis Kahn playing handball off the Great Wall of China, a sad-eyed Buddha contemplating his navel, obviously having no ball, and another depicting two giant mastiffs with the remains of a Baptist minister in their cruel jaws, which Bond guessed was a depiction of the Boxer Rebellion.

"I," began his captor, "am the son of a Singapore opium merchant, Nu Nu, who sold the flower juice of happiness from his boat outside the jurisdiction of the British harbor police. The craft was known throughout all Southeast Asia as 'Nu Nu's Junk Junk.' My father, whilst on a business trip to London, fell in love with a buxom English music hall dancer, Tessie Watts; bedded with her. I am the illegitimate product of that night of shame, named for both of them. My name is Watts Nu.

"My father hated me from birth when the evidences of my mother's lineage, the unslanted eye, the blond hair, began to crop up on my body. I spent a dismal childhood, scorned by people of both races... a *chi-chi*, as the British call half-breeds... an outcast. Though he loathed me, my father, traditionally responsible as all Chinese fathers are, did see to all my wants and had me educated at the Jean Hersholt College of Medicine in Hopei. So highly was I regarded by my professors that they convinced the DuPont Corporation to underwrite my experiments with a new type of chemical aphrodisiac which even today is selling by the millions. You have no doubt purchased it yourself upon occasions. Erectex?"

"Yes," said Bond. "With the slogan 'Better Loving Through Chemistry.' Go on, Doctor, I now find your story fascinating."

That's it, Bond, use your chicken noodle. Flatter this maniac; gain precious time to figure a way out.

"But mere wealth meant nothing to me, Mr. Bond. One thing alone kept me groping through a hostile environment that denied me love, affection and understanding—the thought of revenge. Revenge upon my father, my mother, the whole rotten structure of mankind."

"Was there no one to give you sympathy?" asked Bond, genuinely touched despite his predicament. "There are many fine therapists who might have helped you make an adjustment, find some beauty and meaning."

"Charlatans! Amateurish dabblers in a mystery too profound for their shallow minds! But there was one," and a strange mist came over those incongruous eyes, "who might have helped. I poured out my heart, my frustration, my fears in a thirty-eight-page letter to her. A letter that began 'Dear Abby'... and when she did not deign to answer," his voice rose to a crescendo of fury, "I knew I had squandered my valuable time on a moment of weakness! I pulled up stakes and came to this island where I purchased this broken-down pagoda and turned it into a resort for hate groups, wisely deducing there was a market for this kind of enterprise. At last there is a place where the world's malcontents, with whom I feel a camaraderie, can come for two weeks at a time and rest up for their campaigns. It also serves as an excellent front for a terror organization—"

"SPECTRE," Bond said.

"Ah, you have overheard something you should not have. But it will be of no benefit to you, Mr. Bond. Yes, that is the name. And it is headed by an unique individual whom I met in..." he paused, "I don't think I'll tell you where... but it was a year ago. He is an acknowledged master in the intelligence field and I defer to him because of his organizational genius. His hatred of mankind surpasses even mine, my friend, and together we have made a joint pact. Our goal comes nearer with each passing day."

"What is that goal, Dr. Nu?"

"To rule the world, what else? And we shall! Our organization consists of three-man teams in key spots in every land, people who are totally corrupt and ruthless, who believe as my leader and I do. Among them are three top television executives and three professional football scouts in America, three used car dealers in Canada, three ex-members of Mosley's fascist party in Great Britain, three South African penny whistle players in Jo'burg, a trio of French waiters in Lyons, three rapacious ski instructors at Saint Moritz, three scientists who defected from Red China and are working on a bomb with the destructive force of one hundred wontons (Bond shuddered)... but I could go on all night."

"Have you ever considered that your Communist paymasters have their own vision of world domination and might not take too kindly to you if they found out about yours?"

Dr. Nu's smile was one of superior unconcern. "That possibility has been considered. But they do not know of the scope and purpose of our organization and believe we are content to foment these insurrections for mere money. They are unaware of the bomb we soon will have at our disposal and our even more powerful weapon, the world's most formidable army which I have created. You have already been thwarted by their espionage."

"The insects?"

"Yes, you see..."

There was a scream and two of the sinister Oriental guards came into the room, a struggling hooded figure dragged between them.

"A snooper, Dr. Nu, discovered by one of our centipede sentinels outside the temple," said one with deference.

"You see," Dr. Nu chuckled. "Our allies are ubiquitous, Mr. Bond. Let us see who has blundered into our net." And he lifted the hood.

It was —Sister Sweetcakes!

"Sister, you sweet fool! I told you to go back to OLEO! Take your hands off her, you damn yellow swine!"

"Release her. She cannot cause us harm," the doctor stated placidly.

"Mr. Bond," she started; then let go a sob. "I could not let you face this alone." And buried that ethereal face in her hands.

Dr. Nu looked at her for a moment. "Your entrance, Sister, coincides with one of my daily rituals, not as devout as yours, perhaps, but far more interesting. It is time to make Herbie happy."

"Herbie?" Bond hoped the doctor would not sense the alarm in his query.

"Yes, one of my dearest friends from a singularly isolated sector of jungle in the heart of the Amazon Basin. But come let us meet Herbie, dear guests."

A guard's cutters nipped off the biting strands of Anaconda Copper wire that bound his legs to the chair. (And I own fifty shares of the damn stuff, he thought, with justifiable bitterness.) He felt the blood slowly circulating again, squeezed his toes together to facilitate the process.

They were led by the guard and their giant host down a dark corridor; then up a winding flight of stairs to a door marked "Laboratory."

It opened to reveal a gleaming white laboratory. There were lab tables containing test tubes of various sizes, complicated machinery, something Bond took to be a computer, and a huge circular conference table topped with vases of heady jungle flowers.

"I shall explain that machine to you shortly, Mr. Bond, after we pay our respects to Herbie."

At the end of the laboratory was a door. "It is quite aromatic in there, my friends, but you will become accustomed to it quickly."

He opened it. They were in a huge greenhouse, moist and laden with the pungent smells of rain forest plants of which there were an exotic variety.

"This," said Dr. Nu, pointing to a green snake of a rope potted and tied to a long stick, "is the Malaysian death vine which claimed one of your Israelis, I believe. The genus *tutti cammarata,* as it is known in Latin. Do not go near the thorns. You have already witnessed their efficacy. They pierce the skin, injecting a derivative of the *larosa semolina* toxin. And this—" he bent to pick up a small clay pot—"holds a tiny species of Jamaican flora called the night-blooming day shade. From its seeds can be made a drug that draws the color out of the skin, nerves, and vital organs, a necessary first step toward achieving the state of invisibility. There is a minor drawback, however. The bones are turned kelly green. The only practical use I have discovered for it as yet is selling skeletons for Irish Halloween parties. And," the round eye twinkled to its slanted partner, "here is Herbie."

It was a plant, even taller than the doctor, and, as they approached it, it came alive! Several leaf-covered tendrils began a seductive swaying as though they were the enticing arms of a belly dancer.

"This is as close as all of us but one shall get," said the doctor.

"All right," Bond said. "It should be dancing at the Roundtable. *Nu,* Dr. Nu? I'm getting sick of this charade."

"I could not agree with you more, Oy Oy Seven," Dr. Nu said. "But Herbie's accomplishments go beyond simple manipulations of his handsome arms. Herbie is, incidentally, a nickname. His full moniker, as they say in those cowboy and Indian thrillers, is *herbis homnis fressoris...* man-eating plant."

From somewhere deep in Herbie's green depths came a rumble... and something that sounded like a slurp!

"He knows why we are here, Mr. Bond."

"Oh." Sister sagged in the arms of the guards. "Let it be me—not him. Let it be me."

Bond's voice was a tremulous choke. "All right, take her away and get it over with, you fiend! Don't subject her to any more of this."

"But, Mr. Bond." The polished voice held a note of surprise. "You completely misunderstand. I am going to take Sister up on her offer. It is she who will furnish Herbie with his banquet tonight. I have something subtler in mind for you." He turned to the guards. "Throw her in!"

"I'll kill you all, you—" Bond roared, a red ray of anger across his eyes. He closed the fingers of his bound hands into one fist, brought it up savagely under the jaw of one of the Orientals, experiencing a sweet fierce joy as the fist drove the man's teeth through his tongue. The other, however, had side-stepped his desperate rhinolike charge and brought the butt of his Wembly-Vicar automatic against Bond's head. Oy Oy Seven fell woozily on all fours, felt himself being dragged out of the greenhouse, knees rubbed raw by the Armstrong mosaic title floor.

His last, despairing look was on Sister. Screaming, she was enveloped in three of Herbie's tentacles, a primordial sucking sound coming from heaven alone knew what part of that revolting anatomy.

Then the door shut. And there was only Dr. Nu, arms folded, eyes aglow with a dreamy madness as her screams grew fainter, then ceased.

14
Summit
Conference

There were new bonds for Bond now. The wire was gone; in its stead were Fibreglas straps around his wrists, chest, and legs restraining him in a high-backed chair. Electric? No, I can't believe this is the subtlety to which the maniac alluded. There's something a damn sight more devilish in that crazed brain.

The room was the white laboratory adjoining the greenhouse where adorable Sister Sweetcakes... but there's nothing to be gained by thinking about her now, he reasoned. Steel yourself, buddy boy, it's your turn.

His wounds had been dressed (modishly, in the latest Johnson & Johnson flesh-toned Band-Aids) by the doctor, who apparently had lost none of his medical skill. Dr. Nu reclined in a contour chair of Skelton-Red leather set in the center of the circular conference table. A bottle of Ballantine, the spirited beer, was at his side; he took frequent gulps from it and drags from the tube of a carved ivory hookah, blowing out three connected rings at a time. Topjob, who shot malicious glances at Bond, knelt at his master's feet, rubbing them with Dixie Peach Pomade.

"You are to be accorded a rare privilege, Mr. Bond, and this is because I have learned to hold you in utmost respect for your courage and derring-do. Singlehandedly you have killed three of my security force, wounded several others. But your foolhardy foray into my affairs was doomed from the start."

"What is this privilege, Dr. Nu?"

"That of witnessing my unparalleled genius. I want you to meet another friend of mine, one of my own making." A yellow index finger pointed to the computer, which stood like a silent soldier, its memory banks and switches ready to do its master's bidding. "This is IPECAC."

"What?" Bond's ears refused to believe what he had heard.

"Insect Programmed Electronic Computer for Analyzing Conversation. In short, Mr. Bond, I can talk to insects."

"Now I know you're mad, Dr. Nu. I am willing to admit that 'bugging the bugs' is a unique method of obtaining information. One would never suspect the wayward roach, the frolicking June bug to be spies. But—"

A slight nuance of contempt crossed that composed face. "Mr. Bond, you are tough, resourceful, and clever... up to a point. Yet your mind fails to comprehend the spheres in which my work leads me. I shall give you a demonstration that will save me thousands of words."

He flicked a red switch. A light glowed; Bond's ears suddenly felt a sharp pain, heard an unearthly electronic atonality. "You will find the pain subsiding in a few seconds as your ears adjust to the frequency." He spoke into a microphone. "Sectional commanders will report to the conference table on the double!"

I am as *tzoodrayt* as this yellow Eiffel Tower of a nut, Bond told himself. I must be. I see a parade creeping over the floor, a line of insects! Crawling, hopping, flying low. I hear humming, chirping, buzzing... they're making their way up the legs of the conference table, aligning themselves in set positions... the doctor has pushed another switch... miniature microphones are popping out in front of each bug... and name plates... "JAPANESE BEETLE," "CICADA," "LOCUST," "MOSQUITO," "TSETSE FLY"....
Gottenu! This looks like an insect—

"Summit conference, Mr. Bond," said Dr. Nu with a pleased smile. "That is what you're thinking, isn't it? Before we proceed with the agenda, I'll just"—he turned off the red switch—"cut the frequency so they cannot hear us. In précis, here is the theory that led me to this marvelous discovery and IPECAC.

"As you know, I am a scientist, the world's greatest, you now must concede. As a friendless unwanted child I spent countless lonely hours. Time hung heavy upon my hands, but even at that stage I possessed a boundless intellectual curiosity about my environment. I spent many hours stretched out upon the carpet of the great forest observing nature's littlest creatures scuttle about, make love, kill, die. And I began to notice that all of them would pause momentarily in the presence of their own or other species to move their feelers, antennae, palpi or rub their legs together. This, I deduced, was some kind of language based on sound. Sound that could be heard, as in the case of the crickets; sound that couldn't, i.e., worms, beetles, aphids, termites, etc. Since various insects made certain moves, displayed certain attitudes in the presence of others, I further reasoned there must be an insect Swahili, a lingua franca, known to all such creatures. It was an interesting theory but one I put aside in some dark recess of my mind for future reference. Three years ago I recalled it; launched a series of experiments to validate it. The key word, let me repeat, was 'sound.' Yet, as I stated previously, not all of their sounds were audible, at least to my normal aural range. So I hit upon the felicitous idea of using the most sensitive sound reproduction equipment ever assembled, which could not only discern sound thousands of decibels below human hearing but boost it to our level. You will be surprised to learn that the only equipment capable of this most delicate pickup and boost is to be found solely in the chassis of a 1949 Muntz television set. Now that I could distinguish the sound I began to observe, as I had in my childhood, the different moves of insects, correlating sound and action, until I discovered the fact that though each insect had its own distinct sound it also had a universal one. Thus I began to construct their common language after many months of observing, note-taking, cataloguing. And IPECAC was born. It can do many things, Mr. Bond, because its memory banks have been fed enormous quantities of information about the major orders of insecta. IPECAC hears, reproduces sound to my level, feeds sound to its banks, translates into all major human tongues—I have pressed the English one for your benefit and mine—and reverses the procedure when I wish to communicate with them. But I will show you." Switch back on, he cried: "Hello, little friends!"

Israel Bond thought, I'm mad for sure. For in response to the doctor's salutation he saw the waving and scraping of insect appendages commence in unison; heard them—sing!

"Hippity hop, hutsut, rainbow roo,
Siboneyeh skippity, we love you.
What 'ere you ask we'll gladly do,
'Cause we sure love you, Dr. Nu."

Unbelievable! Scores of insects chanting a childish doggerel to a beloved Romper Room teacher! What's next? he wondered. Will they pull out tiny copies of *My Weekly Reader* and find out if Dick and Jane are pummeling Baby? And that Spot has rabies? And has been making it with Robin Hound?

"Thank you, my creatures," said the doctor benignly. "And now we shall open our seminar with a discussion of how you can help your dear doctor and his leader take over this earth. First, may we hear the scout reports?"

The lighted name plate "HONEYBEE" went on. "I have been buzzing around the convent, Dr. Nu. The Israelis have been given shelter by the monks. They are without weapons, ripe for attack."

"Excellent!" cried Dr. Nu. "I shall contact the main Chinese, Fidelista and Russian Forces in EET and order them to infiltrate tomorrow night across The Band. They will launch a three-pronged attack and wipe out the remaining Israelis and the convent as well. These sanctimonious swine have been a stumbling block and a divisive influence with their insidious good deeds."

HONEYBEE flashed again. "Doctor, I have a distressing personal problem. These continual long-range spy flights have decimated me. My wings are worn to a frazzle, my strength gone."

"Fly over here, little friend," Dr. Nu said kindly, and HONEYBEE made a waspline toward him. "Here," he opened his hand and placed a pill in its palm with the other. "Eat this. A vitamin to restore your health."

"What did you give it?"

"What else, Mr. Bond? Bee-complex."

"Of course."

Now there was a beep as name plate "TICK" lit up. "Doc, will you please tell that goddam CANTHARIS to keep his horny legs off me? You think he gives a crap for our conference? To him it's just an excuse to ball, ball, ball...."

"CANTHARIS, please desist from these unwholesome activities at once!" the doctor ordered.

"Doc," CANTHARIS pleaded. "I got this Spanish fly built in. Can I help it?" And the voice grew suggestive. "Hey, GRASSHOPPER, that's a sweet leg you got there. Let me bite it, baby."

Bond heard a scream from GRASSHOPPER. "Please... no! No!" Dr. Nu's forefinger poked a button. There was a puff of smoke.

The "CANTHARIS" name plate and microphone disappeared. "I regret the disruption," said the doctor, "but we all will agree that CANTHARIS, due to no fault of his own, had to be eliminated. Such as he have no usefulness in this organization."

SCORPION cut in. "Doc, that Israeli trussed up over there... ain't he the one that squashed my poor cousin, Jethro, a while back? Let me give the murdering bastard the back of my tail... a little sting-a-ding-ding-dingaroonie!"

"Leave his fate to me, my little ally from Durango. I shall see to it that your kind is revenged in full."

"Say, Doc." LOCUST was speaking now, and Bond could detect a touch of wariness, even hostility. "What's in all of this for us? All I can see is we're the patsies... the guys who die like flies, you should pardon the expression, flies, while you get this globe handed to you on a plate."

"I had anticipated that very natural question from one of you," said the doctor with the pleasant air of a lecturer about to make a point. "It is true that I shall benefit from your labors, dear insects, but you, too, stand to do the same. For instance, you, LOCUST, you and your brethren, shackled by a ludicrous tradition, only swarm once every seventeen years. Why, pray tell, waste those sixteen in slumber? A triumph for me insures you a free hand—or wing—every year at mankind's bursting granaries, wheat fields, canebrakes untroubled by meddlesome humans with their killing pesticides. HOUSEFLY, would you not enjoy unfettered flight in any human domicile, knowing that those sticky ribbon deathtraps were gone forever? CARPET BEETLE, think of it... the world's fattest, juiciest woolen rugs, thousands of warehouses filled with them, and all at your disposal. MOTH, would it not give you the most exhilarating sensation to gorge yourself on Jerry Lewis' three hundred mohair suits? You see, we have a mutuality of interest here."

"I cannot agree to this thing."

Shocked, all eyes, human and insect, focused on the illuminated name plate "JAPANESE BEETLE."

"Prease to accept humbre aporogy, but cannot be a party to destruction of my beroved Dai Nippon. I go now in peace, yiss, Dr. Nu?"

The answer was a terse, "No."

JAPANESE BEETLE met the same fate as CANTHARIS. A yell of agony, the sickening odor of singed beetle flesh, and it was over. "That also was necessary," the doctor sighed. "If there are no further items, we shall conclude with the singing of our stirring anthem, 'Larva Come Back to Me.'"

As the insects propped themselves up into a humanlike posture of attention and shrilled their song, Bond's thoughts were off his pain-racked body. That computer! If only I could get to it! The seed of a scheme was germinating in his brain.

Dr. Nu watched his horde slink and fly off.

"Can you deny now, Oy Oy Seven, that you, indeed, have been accorded a rare privilege?"

"No. I suppose I shall pay for it in some equally diabolical manner, eh, Dr. Nu?"

"Yes, Israel Bond. Your moment has come." And he clapped his hands. "Topjob! Activate the WC!"

15
David And
Goliath

"Is this to be my fate, Doctor? Drowning by immersion in a water closet? Really, it is unworthy of your salt."

"Silence, unthinking fool! Did you think I would squat to such a plebeian level? WC is yet another device, Mr. Bond. It stands for Will Chiller. I had not planned to destroy that muscular body of yours which seems to have an extraordinarily high tolerance of pain. Besides, I can utilize that body in our organization. You will work your valorous deeds for us, Mr. Bond."

"Never!"

"Oh, yes. But first there is the matter of breaking your indomitable will, bending it to our purposes. And this the Will Chiller will do. Ready it, Topjob."

The doctor's aide grinned wickedly at Bond, revealing bloodied teeth filed to a point. He took something out of his robe pocket and munched on what Bond took to be one of the bat, Masterson's, wings. Then he wheeled over a machine on rollers that seemed to be some sort of television set. On its front was a large glass screen with two large buttons below. One was marked "WD," the other "WR."

"Plug it in, Topjob. I can see you are trying to figure out the abbreviations, Mr. Bond. The first is 'Will Destroyer.' When it is switched on and the subject exposed to the images its built-in tapes bring to the screen, that unhappy person will find his senses departing from him in five minutes. At that juncture, the power is cut off because any further exposure would leave the subject a useless mental vegetable. WR is 'Will Restorer,' built into the machine for my own personal use while I was testing the system. It saved my own life, Mr. Bond, when I carelessly let myself be exposed too long. With my last microdot of sanity I pushed it and became rational again. But we are wasting time. Topjob... the WD button, please."

A pinpoint of light danced on the screen; then spread into a white intensity that flooded away the black.

"Shucks, Jed Clampett. You don't mean ter tell me thar's oil in that thar land?" The speaker on the screen was a scraggly-haired woman in a calico dress. Her question was followed by howls of laughter, from an unseen audience. "What's so funny about that? Bond wondered. "Yup," said a rural-type man with a sunburned face. More uncontrollable laughter; another puzzlement to Bond. "Well, I guess we-uns is rich!" chortled the woman, smacking her backside with a good-natured flourish. More audience laughter; one of the women was shrieking at the top of her lungs.

It faded, supplanted by a pert snub-nosed charmer whose moist lips kept repeating: "Dippity-Do.... Dippity-Do.... Dippity-Do."

From another world he heard Dr. Nu: "One minute."

Now the face on the screen was that of a jolly, bespectacled little man in a pin-stripe suit and straw hat. "What makes you think you're worthy of being our Queen of Misery today, Mrs. Ruth Kurtzer of Buzzard's Bladder, North Dakota, any more than Mrs. Ray Abney, our hunchback from Rufus Jarman, Tennessee, or Mrs. Hilda Shivers, the plucky but hopelessly braindamaged housewife from Cooze Corners, Maine?" "Well, I'll tell yer, Mr. Nelson... I crawled here on muh arthritic legs all the way from Dakoty, with them cars runnin' over my poor chilblained hands, jes' so's I could tell yuh about my spavined son, Chesley, who is feelin' po'ly and needs an operation real bad so's he can harvest the crops in time to make the mortgage payment to hard-hearted Squire Taliaferro." "What do you think, audience?" cried the little man. "Is she the queen?" Booing and catcalling broke out; a brick thrown on-stage smashed the woman in her old grey head. "Guess not," shrugged the little man. "Let's bring on our last contestant, Mrs. Louise Wieczorek of Chauquatauchauqua, Oklahoma, our thalidomide-taking mother who fears that..."

"Two minutes," said Dr. Nu, inhaling his hookah tube.

An emotion-packed voice. "Yes, this fall you'll thrill to the dramatic series of a man searching for himself, Shelley Keats,

a new face that will haunt your memory forever, in the role of
Flapjack Huggins, a Texas medico-scuba diver with amnesia and
incurable conjunctivitis, falsely accused of leaving his comrades
to die in the Alamo, a Dallas motel, in 1959. Ride, walk, and swim
with Flapjack Huggins and his laughable side-kick, Waco, as he
seeks for thirty-nine or seventy-eight episodes the man who
smeared his name. Thrill to every episode of *Branded Forgetful
Underwater Intern Who Rides, Walks and Swims for His Life.*"

Bond's cruelly handsome face was undergoing a startling
transformation into a clownish moronic simper.

"Three minutes," said Dr. Nu.

"Geez, Gidget." The gawky young teener on the screen fought
to keep the tears from running into his pimples. "You mean you
forgot you promised to go to the prom with me and now you're
going with Barney Kincaide, the smartest, handsomest boy in the
class... even after I drove my hot rod off the cliff to impress you
'n' ever'thing?" More riotous laughter from nowhere. "Well, I...
I..." stammered the pixieish blonde sweetheart of Wollstonecraft
Junior High. "Did I do something wrong, Daddykins, did I?" A
man in a tweed smoking jacket puffed his pipe. "I don't know,
sweetheart. I'm just your schmuck of a father. Ask mommy. She
knows everything. She'll pull you out of this jam like she does
every week on this matriarchally oriented situation comedy
show."

"Four minutes," said Dr. Nu. Bond's eyes were rolling
around, tongue sliding in-and-out. "You may unbind his hands
now, Topjob; he has been rendered harmless. I don't want him
to lacerate his wrists on his straps in his frenzy."

"Certs is a candy mint." "No, Certs is a breath mint!"

"Let Certs Hertz you in the driver's seat!"

"You mean to say that if the cobalt bomb destroys the world,
you'll still cover my losses? H-m-m, John Hancock, huh?"

"How'd you like a nice Hawaiian punch?" Pow! "Fruit juicy,
fruit juicy, Dippity Do, Dippity Do..."

The face of Bond was frozen into a mindless ear-to-ear grin.
His thumb was on his nose, four fingers waving in cadence. He
was humming "The Doublemint Gum" song.

"Ten seconds more, Topjob, and Secret Agent Israel Bond
will be our unwitting tool."

With a sob and a rush of breath a hooded figure leaped
between them; jammed a finger into the WR button.

On the screen—a handsome man in a well-cut Jackie Gordon suit, his face full of urbanity, tenderness, intelligence, wit—all the qualities present in the best of Twentieth Century man—smiled: "Good evening. This is *Open End* and my name is David Susskind. Our panel discussion tonight is on the subject, 'Will Automation, Carried to the Extreme, Throw Millions of Computers Out of Work?,' and to probe this unique problem of our times I have asked the following panelists to appear tonight—Leonard Bernstein, Arthur Fiedler and the entire Boston Pops Orchestra, Nipsey Russell, Arlene Francis and, for comedy relief, Hugh Downs."

From the first outpourings of that mellifluous, cultured voice of sweet reason, Bond had felt the horrible banalities of button *WD* fleeing his brain like frightened Lucky Thompson gazelles in the path of a Kenya brush fire. And those intellectual names! Bernstein! Francis! Russell! Each one a torch of truth and knowledge, burning away his torpor.

He was a steely spring again, lashing out with cast-iron hands on the jaws of the nonplussed Topjob, sending the killer karateist crashing into the wall.

A cold grey eye snapped a photo of the enraged Dr. Nu struggling with the slight hooded figure who had saved Bond from insanity. He battered the doctor's midsection, fists flailing with devastating potency. Dr. Nu said, "Ugh!," doubled up in agony and fell over his contour chair.

Bond swept the hooded figure into his arms.

"Israel! Israel!"

He looked down into the face of Sister Sweetcakes!

"My darling! Alive, but—"

"Hurry!" she cried. "We must find a way out!"

He carried her to the first door he could find, slammed it behind him, secured it with a bolt.

"Oh, Israel! You've taken me into the greenhouse again."

"*Gottenu!* We're in another pickle! I hope it's Kosher this time. But, my OLEO angel, how did you escape the clutches of that chlorophyll horror back there?" He gazed at Herbie, heard the rumble of hunger. A tentacle shot out, fell a few feet short of his leg.

He could hear a groan of frustration. "Eat your heart of lettuce out, you green son-of-a-bitch!" And to Sister: "You haven't answered me, my nun turned wildcat."

There was a mischievous sparkle in those violet eyes. "Israel, think it out for yourself with that keen mind I admire so."

"I see," Bond nodded. *Herbis homnis fressoris.* Our Celery Cyclops only eats—"

"Men. Just as his generic name states. He really was quite flustered upon discovering I was what I was. Expelled me from his interior in an instant."

"Damn fool, that Herbie." And the grey eyes searched her violet ones and in a burning moment of revelation found something there—the reflection of grey eyes. I shall kiss her now, he told himself; my lips will start to home in on paradise. *Gottenu!* There was a staggering blow on the back of his neck. Sister screamed.

"It's another bug! Oh, heavenly Father... it's enormous!"

Bond spun, fell to the floor just in time to avoid another blow from a thing with the buzz of a light plane motor. A beetle with a horrifying seven-inch circumference and the black hardness of coal! It swooped back, rammed its body against his temple. He somersaulted under a table. Overhead it droned, seeking its prey.

"It's after me, Sister.... Goliath beetle," he panted. "Biggest of its breed. Comes from Africa."

He felt the welts rising on his head and neck. Damn thing has the kick of a mule! And those pincers! They can tear out two inches of flesh!

"Sister," he said tensely. "Give me a handkerchief, *tout de suite!*" * She tossed it to him, fearful eyes looking upward.

Bond reached into his pocket. He found what he had hoped to find. A handful of Israeli coins, five of them, three *agorot* and two *escargot.*

He folded the handkerchief into a triangle, grabbed one point in his right hand, put the five coins in the fold. Then he drew himself up boldly.

"Come, Goliath. A son of the House of David awaits thee."

Buzz-z-z-z-z! A sound from the far corner.

It was ready to meet his brazen challenge. Down it zipped in a black blur. Round and round swung tho muscular arm of Israel Bond. The Goliath was coming fast now... ten feet away... nine... eight... seven... six....

Five coins left the improvised sling, slicing through the air like tracer bullets strafing a train. They crunched into the

---

*   Sound your horn for the Sucaryl.

Goliath. Two buried themselves in its back, smashing through the hard shell, biting deeply into its insides. One ripped off a leg; two more chipped out eyes with their ridged edges.

It fell to the floor with a thump, flopping about madly. Bond, his rage abated now, stubbed out the last vestige of its life.

He turned to Sister, whose eyes were filled with candid adoration.

"Borrowing a term from your old days in jazz, Sister: when it comes to fighting a Goliath, it don't mean a thing if you ain't got that sling!"

16
Rotten Roger:
The Last Call

"The door! It's glowing!" she wailed.

"Damn it!" Bond growled. "While I'm giving myself the *Croix de guerre*[*] those babies out there are still at it."

They backed off, watching the metal of the door change from dun gray to pink, to a warm red, to a hotter white. The heat rolled over them like a Saharan wind.

"They're using acetylene torches on the metal. They'll be through in another minute. Sister, this way!" He picked up the table and flung it through the glass wall of the greenhouse. "Through that hole on the double!"

She passed through the ragged opening which caught at her habit, tearing it.

Content that she was safe for the nonce, he stood halfway between the door and the back wall, tensing his battered body.

With a shower of sparks the door fell.

Two of the guards rocketed through, made a grab for him. Bond lurched to the side. Their momentum carried them by him. He turned to face their next rush but they did not charge back.

They had gone too far beyond him! And into the grasp of Herbie!

He shuddered as he watched them vainly trying to free themselves of those greedy arms. One was lifted high into the air kicking and screeching; then dropped into the loathsome depths. He heard a crunch, saw two boots and a helmet spat out.

---

[*] Star of David.

Bond picked up the man's carbine and put his partner out of his misery. Better a bullet than....

Gottenu! Something smashed into his arm; the carbine was sent clattering to the floor!

Topjob!

Fool that I am, I turned my back. Now my arm is dangling like a subway strap. I must combat this mass of Oriental sinews with one swollen arm.

The karateist circled Bond with a malevolent grin, those pointed teeth clicking with excitement, the mouth slobbering for the kill. He'll make it a slow job, a top job, will Topjob, Bond knew. Crack every bone in my body with one well-placed chop after another to the vulnerable spots.

One chance! Back slowly away, Oy Oy Seven... slowly... let him advance inch by inch, savoring every moment of your fear... your whimpering is as delicious to this ape as a mouthful of leeches or a bat's entrails... "ooooh"... that's it... moan a little... his grin is widening... you're almost there, but for God's sake as soon as you feel the first prick—freeze! And pray to the Lord of Israel that your shirt is thick enough to keep the tip from going into your epidermis....

His back made contact with the tip.

"All right, Topjob, do your worst, you f— gook!"

Topjob snarled and made his run at Bond. His hand speared into Bond's shoulder as the Israeli leaped to the left. The karate specialist's follow-through sent him sprawling into the Malaysian death vine!

Bond gnashed his teeth as the pain spread through his torn shoulder. He opened his eyes and met those of the Korean, whose own were slowly being overcome by dullness. Topjob's hand moved toward Bond's neck. It's the moment of truth, thought Bond. Has he got enough left to deliver the final death chop to my esophagus? If he has, I can't stop it.

The hand brushed Bond's neck but the blow was powerless. Topjob started to fall slowly like an oak severed from its base by a handsaw. He tumbled to the floor, shook in a cataclysmic paroxysm and lay still.

Bond rolled the Korean on his back with a shove of his foot. From his armpit to his thigh Topjob was pierced with a row of thorns.

Sister Sweetcakes had quietly returned through the crack in the glass wall. "Israel. What... what happened to this man?"

He fished into his lapel pocket with his usable arm; stuck a Raleigh into his lips.

"Topjob was tough all right, Sister... damn tough. But he ran into a Jew who was a thorn in his side."

"Oh, Father in heaven, you're hurt again!" she cried. "Your arm..."

"Broken, I'm afraid. But there's no time for tears now, Sister. I've a little date with that machine in the next room."

She helped him make his way into the lab. "This is IPECAC, Sister. What it does I'll explain later. But don't think me dotty when I talk to it. I know what I'm doing. Flick that red switch. And when I stop talking, flick it off."

She complied.

Bond spoke into the microphone. "Attention, Rotten Roger, my leader. Those stupid insects are prepared to follow my instructions blindly. They will help us take over the world. Then when they have accomplished our task for us, I shall destroy them to the last bug! Ha-ha! The fools! They do not know that I, Dr. Watts Nu, have invented an insecticide so potent that it makes Black Flag and Raid seem like Breakstone Cream Cheese. Roger, Rotten Roger, and out." tie dragged on the Raleigh again. "That should crack the unholy alliance wide open. Every bug within five miles has heard Dr. Nu's plan for betrayal. Now, to find the man behind all this, Leader Colfax."

They trod the corridor lightly, Sister in the lead steering the limping secret agent as best she could. She again felt that disturbing electricity as his long tapering fingers enclosed hers.

In the darkness Bond stumbled, banged his torn shoulder into the wall.

There was an ear-piercing ring.

"Damn it! The wall... it's wired to set off an alarm when touched. We're in for it again, Sister."

At the other end of the corridor a door opened and three of the Orientals came tramping through.

"Sister, run! I can't make it! Save your pretty neck."

"No, Israel," she whispered hotly. "Try, please try...."

She yanked at his sleeve and they began to run. As they traversed the corridor they saw a number of doors with slivers of light winking out. "These must be the rooms rented by the Temple of Hate to its vacationing clientele," she said. "Quickly... into this one!"

They found themselves in the rear of a large dimly lit hall. In the front was a hideous potbellied idol with red eyes that bored into their very souls. A little man with a messianically maddened face sat in the cross-legged style of the East, addressing a group of dark-hued men in loincloths.

"Oh, my brothers! I have good omens for you. Last night a jackal cried on my left, a baboon defecated on my right. They are a sign for us mother Thuggees who have lain asleep for, lo! these past fifty years. Rise again! Take up your strangling cords and kill!

> *"Kill lest ye be killed yourselves!*
> *Kill for the love of killing!*
> *Kill for the love of Kali!*
> *Kill! Kill! Kill!"*

The nun shook. "Israel, who are these people?"

"Thugs. The murder cult of India. They worship Mother Kali, goddess of blood. Look! See their leader? He is about to offer Mother Kali a sacred golden melon in homage. Listen, he's going to chant the centuries-old ritual to her."

They strained their ears and caught the thin reedy voice of the high priest kneeling before the idol with the melon in his outstretched palms.

> *"Here's another melon, Kali, baby,*
> *Cuddle up and don't be blue...."*

Bond nudged Sister. "Let's get the hell out of here."

They were back in the corridor. There was a guttural cry in Chinese. A guard had observed the sudden burst of light in the corridor and was shouting for reinforcements.

"Into this room." Bond said. And they pushed open another door.

The sign on the Speaker's rostrum read:

> *DON'T BUY POLISH HAMS!*
> *DON'T EAT HUNGARIAN GOULASH!*
> *DON'T LISTEN TO JAPANESE RADIOS!*

"Good evening, friends of the Western Colorado Chapter of the Vigilante Defenders. My name is Robert Forrest, the national chairman, your keeper of the flame." The tall rickety-thin man waved a greeting. He wore a green-and-white Sears seersucker suit, a white shirt with brown stripes, red-and-blue tie with a painting of Trigger, Roy Rogers' stallion, on the front, Army-Navy Store khaki socks and Father & Son brown brogues.

"It is wonderful to see so many fresh, fine, smiling American faces imbued with the fervor for the Vigilante Defenders' philosophy of life. You know, I've been involved with VD for many years now... I think VD, I sleep with VD, I try to spread VD... and in the course of many travels across our great country, from the towering skyscrapers of New York... 'course some of us have good reason to call it Jew York..." his audience tittered... "to the sunny shores of Californigh-ay, where things are so liberal out there that you can't even call a spade a spade,"... boisterous laughter and prolonged clapping... "in my travels I've noticed the evil fingers of the Communist octopus extending into every American home. Did you know, dear VDers, that many of the toys our blessed tots play with are made by—Marx? Here's a little truck in my hand..."

"Enough," said Bond.

"I think so," Sister agreed.

Back into the corridor. "Let's try this door." Bond opened a third; it squeaked loudly. The room was very small. A naked bulb cast a pale yellow light on the shabby walls. Little piles of plaster dotted the floor.

"Oh, you must help me! You must!" A huge, truck driver of a hand was crushing Bond's throbbing shoulder. "My name is Lawrence Talbot."

He was a large powerful man with a sad yet appealing type of horse face. He wore a dirty white shirt open at the collar, slacks held up by a knotted rope. He was in his bare feet.

"How can I help you, sir?" said a sympathetic Bond.

"There is a curse on me," the man said in a morose voice. "Soon the moon will be full..."

"It is now," Sister said helpfully.

"Oh no!" He sat on his unmade bed, his head in his hands. They heard his muffled voice; saw his shoulders shaking. "I have the mark of the beast upon me. When the moon is full I become one myself and kill! kill! kill!"

"You'd be a hit two doors down. Ever think of becoming a Thug?"

"Don't laugh at me! You don't believe me. Nobody believes me," the anguished man croaked.

"I—uh—rather think I do." Bond was edging toward the door, Sister's hand in his. He had seen the man's finger- and toe-nails growing. "Incidentally, I'll stop around when you're feeling better, Mr. Talbot. I'll give you the address of a fine gypsy woman in Vasaria. Name's Maleva. She knows about these things. Quick, Sister!"

He pulled her roughly out into the corridor and slammed the door into the face of the man, who had charged off the bed, his bared canines framed in a mask of hair.

"Well, none of these doors has gotten us anywhere."

"There is another one, Israel. With a gold star on it at the far end."

They approached it cautiously. Bond's heart pounded as he saw the sign. Journey's end!

"ROTTEN ROGER COLFAX."

And underneath: "Society for Promulgating Every Conceivable Type Of Rottenness."

Israel Bond let a sneer curl his lips. "Sister, you're looking at the bloodiest fool who ever walked down the pike. I let my romantically-febrile imagination lead me down the garden path. I am guilty of ignoring the obvious for the fanciful."

He put his ear to the door.

"... payable in cash or equivalent value in diamonds, Premier Chou. Our organization will see to it that the American geologists are constantly harassed. Killed, if need be. Thus, the way will be paved for your People's Republic of China to be greeted with open arms. You are agreed to these terms? Capital! This is Rotten Roger Colfax—"

"Signing off for the last time." Bond spoke his gritty sentence as he walked through the door. "The game is up, Nochum."

"Bond!"

Sister shrilled, "It's Pablito! What have you done with him, you horrible little man?" She raced to the side of a little boy in raggedy sweater and shorts, whose dried tearstains had formed tributaries on his dirty pinched cheeks. She took a letter opener from Nochum's Allandale mahogany desk, worked it behind the boy's back. "You're free now, little angel," she wept as the strands fell to the floor.

Bond's gray eyes held a gleam of menacing amusement "Nochum, you are no dummy—literally."

Nochum Spector bit his lip, then raised it in a pout of contempt. "That's correct, Mr. Super-Jew with the low-grade wit that everybody's supposed to turn cart wheels for. I had you fooled real good. By now you've guessed that the Vi Teh Minh men placed a replica of me in the pit. I was in the lead; so I simply rode behind a bush, made a few heart-rending noises and they did the rest."

"Yes, they did. They murdered two of your countrymen."

"Hacks! Third-raters! Water boys! They must always perish when they get in a great man's way, Oy Oy Seven. You were my real target; you've always been. But I see that your angel has been sitting on your shoulder again, you lucky, bumbling, overrated, thickskulled—"

"Why, Nochum? Just for the record."

"Why? Remember what you once said to me—'Stay in the playpen. This game's for big boys.' Well, I sure as hell played it like a big boy, Israel Bond. I organized the world's most diabolical terror organization with the help of that wacked-up Chink and his gadgets. I, little bitty Nochum Spector, the forgotten nephew of the great M., the old broad with the wisdom of the ages and that *fahkokteh* chicken soup. Do you know what it meant to be the nephew of M.? How the big shots in M 33 and 1/3, including yourself, laughed at 'poor little Nochum, helpless little Nochum... he'll never get anywhere... he'll ride to his pay check on his *tanteh's* I. J. Fox coattails.' But I fooled you all. Even though I never got the glory assignments and the booze 'n' broads that go with 'em, I wasn't wasting my time. 'Poor little Nochum' was listening, learning and, one day, betraying. Small jobs at first... little tips here and there to Jordan or Syria for a few hundred pounds... then I branched out big in Russia, stung the comrades for a million rubles. Now the Red Chinese are coming through with twenty million *sunyatsens*. And with my Chink No. 2 and his bugs and the wonton bomb I'll make the world grovel at my feet!"

"I could kick myself—"

"I wish the hell you would," snarled Nochum, that baby face puckered into an abhorrent glare.

"I overheard your name mentioned, thought you to be dead and concluded the terror organization in question was spelled S-P-E-C-T-R-E. When I referred to that name in my interesting dialogues with Dr. Nu he naturally thought I was referring to *his* affiliation with the Society for Promulgating Every Conceivable

Type Of Rottenness. Incidentally, what colossal conceit, Nochum! Surely you must have known one of your old section mates would figure out those initials someday."

"By then it would have been too late to matter."

"It's all over now, little man with big dreams."

"Not yet!" And Nochum shot through the floor!

"A chute!" Bond cried. "And here on the desk... a button! The little bastard pressed it while waxing so eloquently. God knows where he is now. We've got to get up to the convent and warn the folks. There's an attack coming. They'll be wiped out in the morning!"

17
Roll, Roll, Roll
Your Ball

After reuniting Pablito with his overjoyed parents in the village of Pupi Campo (Mrs. Garcia covered Bond with tear-soaked kisses of joy; Mr. Garcia shook his hand with awe and picked his pocket), they made their way up Mount Maidenhead on a winding obscure trail known only to Sister Sweetcakes and the Keystone Automobile Club, slipping time and again in hidden mudholes, their faces raked by spiny (though nonpoisonous to Jews and Catholics) *rikki-tikki* shoots.

Once he stopped in his tracks, put a warning finger to his lips. "Mamba." A reptile snaked across their path, followed closely by several smaller ones. "Mamba's Daughters."

At the halfway point to OLEO they heard another melody from the Camp Camp loud-speaker. "Scallopini's Symphony in DC for Congressman and Kickback," he said authoritatively. "The largo de cascara passage has always moved me."

Sister brushed a gila monster off her leg. "Israel, what can we do about the impending attack?"

"I don't know. We have no weapons up there. They'll have mortars, grenade launchers, machine guns. They don't even have to scale the mountain. They can just pop at us from Camp Camp and blow the convent to bits." As though his last sentence had decided something for him, he turned to her, a curious tenderness on his cruelly handsome face. "Sister, I'm not letting you go a step further."

"Israel, I must go back. OLEO is my home."

He was fighting an emotion now, one that made him clench and unclench his fists. His watchband again snapped in two; so did his rolled Bethlehem Steel I.D. bracelet.

"Sister Sweetcakes, I love you. There is no one in this world quite like you, your gentleness, your selflessness... damn it, Sister! Renounce your calling! Renounce your faith and take mine!"

Lashed by a passion he would no longer fight, he told himself: I shall kiss her. Our bodies will lock and sway in a kiss that will teleport us to a golden meadow bending in a warm, murmuring wind, where lambs and lions and friars and optimists and rotarians lie together in peace on the banks of a clear, sweet brook containing natural fluorides whose waters will gurgle "The Indian Love Call."

Eyes closed, sweet surrender written on his dark, cruelly handsome face (in both Hebrew and Latin), his lips sought hers—but found a rigid hand pushing them away. "It can not be, Mr. Bond."

"You called me Israel one otherworldly moment ago. Why this change of heart? Why, why, why?"

"I'll tell you, I'll tell you, I'll tell you," she stammered.

He lit a Raleigh. "Sister, is this to be the farewell speech, the verbal Dear John the Baptist letter?"

"Yes, Mr. Bond. You ask too much of me. Give up my nun's garb; give up my faith. Why did you not ask me to give up my color as well?"

"Actually, you really could. There a an in California by the name of Earl Scheib who promises that for $29.95..." He bit his lip, realizing the horrible option he had just give her. "You know that doesn't mean a damn thing to me. We don't *have* to live in a decent neighborhood."

Her hands fluttered. "At a time like this," she said, "I wish I had not vowed to give up smoking. I have already broken one vow by even thinking of you in a secular way. I shall do penance for it, Mr. Bond, if the cardinal is understanding. Believe this, Mr. Bond. If ever I had again wanted the company of a man, a man's man, it would have been you. What woman could resist that courage, that strength, that passion, and those great one-liners?"

"Manifestly, you are that woman, Sister." His words were tinged with bleakness.

"Yes. And I will tell you why. When I saw the tragic innocence on the face of Pablito, I realized there were so many, many thousands like him on this island, children of the poor who need me more than you do, Mr. Bond. To give them succor I must deny that part of me which is all too human, the part that remembers too well the feeling of personal abandonment with your kind of man."

"Sister,"... the tears were falling like rain on a case of Hunt's Ketchup... "I have been"... his voice faded... "a rotter."

"Oh, no, dear Mr. Bond," and she wiped each one away with the tail of her habit. "For a person who kills as readily as you do, you are the most sensitive tender being I have ever known. Come, let us be firm friends forevermore."

"That would be my dearest wish," said Israel Bond. "But I would ask—no, beg—for one favor."

"Name it, Mr. Bond. It is yours."

"Please, please never mention to another living soul that you saw a secret agent cry."

Dawn came to El Tiparillo, one of many English girls who had taken advantage of the low seasonal rates.

Early risers, the comical *balagoola* birds darted from tree to tree, their raucous "peterpee! peterpee!" rousing the denizens of the jungle. A bull chameleon's sticky tongue scored its first direct hit of the day on an unsuspecting *colavito* fly. Under the canopy of the trees, where no light shone, snorting Gillette razorback hogs dug their tusks under rotted timbers searching for succulent grubs, severing the head and tail and eating just the grubsteaks. The heat, already soaring, caused a fungus mold on a log to burst into pure penicillin. And in a pool, its surface painted brownish-green by algae, a piranha and electric eel thrashed about in a fight to the death, the latter's Ever-Ready battery losing power as they exchanged vicious bites.

Israel Bond stood on the precipice looking down into the Valley of the Blind at the Temple of Hate. His field glasses caught the sun glinting off bayonets and throwing knives. He saw Spector, in the uniform of a field marshal, and Dr. Nu walk into the paved area and the soldiers lift their rifles in salutes. He had counted five hundred of them.

His unrequited love for the nun shoved into a deep corner of his mind from whence he might extract it someday and weep about it into his egg-drop soup, Bond was very much the cold unfeeling Oy Oy Seven again.

A feathery touch on his arm made him turn. Baldroi LeFagel. "Oh, your sweet body is all cut up. Let me rub it down—with mine."

"Damn it, LeFagel! This is no time to flounce around. There are five hundred guys down there who'll be shooting up this place any moment now, guys who can blast the head off a pin, who blend into the jungle and strike like rattlers, who can kill you with one karate stroke."

"Oh, worry not, you heart-stopping thing. I'll protect that precious Herculean body of yours. I have a black belt in karate myself."

"So have they."

"Mine has sequins."

The six survivors of the Israeli Peace Corps, two on crutches, all bearing the scars of the sneak attack, came to the cliff's edge. In their eyes he could see trust and hope. He knew they looked to him for leadership in this hour of tribulation. By thunder, he would give it to them!

He lit a Raleigh; let his eyes rest on each face for a few seconds. "At a time like this when our backs are against the wall, I'd like to pose a simple question: Any of you guys ever hear of George Gipp?"

From the lack of recognition, even disinterest on their faces, he knew he'd taken the wrong tack in resurrecting The Gipper. He would start again, this time with a more whimsical approach.

"*Boochereem,* it looks hopeless. I just learned the convent's telephone line to Vera Hruba has been cut. I can't get through to Bon Ami for men and ammo. But don't despair. I'll get us out of this somehow."

Five of them smiled grimly, but he saw their faces set into masks of determination. Stout lads! They'll give a good account of themselves. But a sixth dropped his crutches, climbed over the low retaining wall girdling the convent and jumped three thousand feet to his death.

"If he's going to show bad faith like that we can bloody well do without him," Bond said stonily. "Brother Thelonius!" The monk looked up from his beloved yellow billyrosebush. "There'll be one less for breakfast."

"Hey!" shouted one of the corpsmen. "We got company! Look, a dozen guys coming up the mountain."

Bond's heart leaped. Could Bon Ami have somehow learned of their plight and sent men and guns? Hot damn! With the right weapons we could hold off that army until real help comes.

Over the wall popped a red sweating face. "Hi, folks! The Rock of Ages Records' caravan is right on the ol' schedule! Tell Sister Sweetcakes to sound her A a few times. Marty O'Marty and the boys are in town!"

Down went his heart, pierced by an arrow of futility. *Gottenu!* Of all the times to record a religious album... with death from international Communism staring us in the face. "We who are about to die salute you, Mr. O'Marty." And taking the recording executive aside he gave it to him straight.

"I better tell the fellas, Mr. Bond." O'Marty beckoned to A Man Called Peter and the Padres, four thick-mopped musicians with Selmer harps, and the technicians who puff up the path bearing the tools of the trade. "It's all off."

"Hey, man?" said A Man Called Peter. "You mean like we ain't havin' no session?"

"Kid, don't you realize that the Vi Teh Minh men, the Russkis and Fidelistas might be here any second?"

"Screw them other groups, daddy. You signed the contract with *us.*"

"I shall personally lead our onslaught upon the convent," said Nochum Spector. "You will be at my side, Dr. Nu. I'm sure it will gladden your heart to see our bullets cut down these dogs."

"There is just one of them who interests me, my leader. Israel Bond. I shall have my revenge upon him. I want him staked out naked on a bed of ground glass in the tropical sun, watch his lidless eyes burned black by its rays, hear his screams for mercy as I place bamboo slivers under his nails and light them."

"I shall leave the fate of the great Oy Oy Seven to you, my good Doctor. Are your insects prepared to soften them up before we move in?"

"I outlined our plan over IPECAC a few minutes ago. They will swarm over and into the convent, biting, tearing, stinging. Our job should be what the Americans call 'shooting fish in a barrel' after that."

"Excellent! Let us move up the mountain. The first barrage is at 1300 hours."

Around the table in the dining hall of OLEO, served by the solicitous nuns and Monks Thelonius and Julius, sat Bond, the Peace Corps boys, Baldroi LeFagel, Dr. Browndorf, and Marty O'Marty's retinue.

"Delicious, absolutely delicious," said the doctor. "What is it, Sister Butterball?"

The plump little nun blushed. "It's what the Americans call 'fish in a barrel.' We nuns put mackerel, holy mackerel, of course, in a barrel and..."

"Bond! I've got my transistor radio working," called out O'Marty. "At least we can get some news of the outside world." He turned a dial. "Hey, a Miami station."

"... identified by White House security men as the leader of the protest against our involvement in Viet Nam was Rowena Rosenthal, eighteen, of Manhattan. Miss Rosenthal said she would urge young men not only to set fire to their draft cards but also to their draft *boards*. And in Viet Nam itself, American B-52's plastered the North Vietnamese hamlet of O Feel Yah for the third straight day. Aerial reconnaissance photos, according to an Air Force spokesman, showed that our bombers—quote—knocked out fifteen thousand trees, which will never again threaten the freedom of the South Vietnamese people, at least six small hills and a very sullen swamp—unquote. From the politically torn island of El Tiparillo comes word of new civil war this morning. West El Tiparillan forces were rushed to The Band, that neutral zone that divides the island, to meet the forces of General Obratsov from EET which launched an attack late last night. Said General Wesson y Oyl of WET—quote—We shall never, never surrender and, if we do, it will be with dignity—unquote. Early stock market reports show Calvert up a fifth, International Nickel down a quarter, International Quarter down a nickel, and Made-A-Wee Diapers unchanged. And that—"

"Turn it off, Marty. We heard the news all right and it's lousy," said Bond. Revolution in El Tiparillo! And WET's army committed to the border. No, there'll be no in-the-nick-of-time cavalry charge for us, Gunga Din.

OLEO shook violently as the first barrage whined over the wall into its side. Nuns screamed, sank to their knees in prayer. Bond looked down at his hand, sliced from heel of palm to pinky tip by a spear of a shell fragment. Dust choked his nostrils. He felt his rubbery legs giving way.

Sister caught him. "Mr. Bond, you're hurt again!"

She tore off a strip of her garment and wound it around his gushing hand. "It's the best I can do, my poor friend."

He patted her hood. "You always do the best you can, Sister. Anybody else hurt?"

"Brother Julius. A slight scratch. But what are we to do?"

"Sister, only God knows. I had not foreseen this hopeless siege. This is not a slickly planned affair with predictable moves and countermoves like Operation Matzohball."

Matzohball!

Say it again, he screamed at his brain. Say it again!

"Matzohball!"

"Brain, you used your head," and he laughed harshly, triumphantly.

"Mr. Bond, you are acting in a highly irrational—"

"Matzohball!" he whooped in a fierce boyish joy. "That's it! Sister," and he hugged the bewildered nun, "have you any large kettles?"

"Kettles? Adversity has at last unhinged you, Mr. Bond. Would you throw kettles at these murderous, heavily armed, godless barbarians?"

"Come, come," Bond chided. "No commercials for our religious beliefs. We both know that God helps him who helps himself. Kettles?"

"Only a small one or two for making tea. The soup and the stews are prepared in the cauldrons."

"Cauldrons! *Oy mommeleh,* cauldrons! Let's get 'em!"

She led him into the kitchen. "There." On top of the old-fashioned stove were a dozen four-foot-deep cauldrons.

"Tell every able hand, man and woman, to get cracking! I want them in here on the double!"

A minute later they stood hushed before him.

"You haven't got time to tell me how crazy I am. You've just got time to do what I tell you to do. I'm going to work all your asses off—pardon me, Sisters and Brothers—and you won't stop. Dear ladies, get me boiling water. And I want every man jack of you to follow me to the cellar. Let's go. It's time to start the ball rolling!"

"I see smoke coming from the roof," said Dr. Nu. "Our last barrage must have set it on fire. We shall not have to wait too long now, leader of SPECTOR, Spector."

Nochum growled. "Where are your insect allies? They should have overrun the place by now."

"Perhaps there has been some misunderstanding, SPECTOR leader. But I feel sure—"

"Misunderstanding?" Spector's voice was icy. "You know what the penalty is for failing SPECTOR."

Dr. Nu almost turned white. "My leader, I'm sure that—wait! Listen! Tell the men to stop firing."

Spector held up his hand. The shooting stilled.

"Hist!" cried Dr. Nu. "Can you not hear them?"

From far off they heard a drone. One solid sound at first. And then, as it came nearer, they could distinguish individual noises, buzzing, chirping, the crackling of dead leaves under billions of insect feet. Now, there unfolded a black blanket, spreading over the horizon as far as the eye could see. Uncountable hordes of ants, scorpions, tarantulas, crickets, beetles, centipedes... all manner of crawling things... and, hovering above them, their winged cousins in air-borne legions that for an instant blotted out the sun.

"They are coming to me," Dr. Nu smiled.

"It's quiet down there," said Dr. Browndorf. "Something's fishy."

Bond put down his field glasses. "No, buggy. Look, Doc."

The medico put them to his eyes. "My God, bugs! Ugh! Billions 'n' billions 'n' —"

"Don't get panicky, Doc. I've a feeling they won't be coming here after all. Are the boys doing the job?"

"Yes. The cauldrons are lined up by the wall. And one of the boys got a brainstorm. He tore down all the rain spouts, tied them together and formed a sort of pipeline to the kitchen. We'll get a continual supply of hot water from the hot water taps."

"*Tov m'oad!* And the stuff?"

"They're opening it and boiling it as fast as they can."

"Make sure it's packed as tight as a witch's tit. Use just enough hot water to make it firm and bouncy. A soggy one won't go fifty feet."

"Roger."

"Don't ever say that name again," Bond said savagely. "It's lost its charm." Idiot! You had to open your sensual mouth! Now the doc's looking oddly at you. Can he suspect that M.'s own nephew is a traitor? No, of course not. Nobody knows but you and Sister. And it must stay that way out of respect to the grandest old dame you'll ever know.

"Oy Oy Seven!"

Bond's morbid spell was broken by one of the Israeli boys coming up the path, running, in fact, from Baldroi LeFagel who nimbly skipped after him.

"Baldroi, leave the kid alone or I'll—"

LeFagel said gaily, "Look, it's all over my hands." He held them out, revealing a gummy yellow covering. "I've been helping those *superb* young men pack it. I tasted it, incidentally. It's delicious. Jewish delicacy, no? But then all Jewish delicacies taste delicious. You're Jewish, aren't you, Bond?"

Bond sent the little poet spinning with a backhanded cuff. "Get lost, you— or I'll tan your hide. Uh—sorry, LeFagel."

"You had to make it a racial issue, right, Whitey?"

The young Israeli, whose name was Neon Zion, said, "We're ready to roll, Oy Oy Seven. Give us the word."

They were silent as he approached them, even the nonstop talker, O'Marty.

"Did you knock out a big enough section of the retaining wall?"

"Didn't have to," piped up Brother Thelonius. "They did it for us with their last mortar barrage."

"O.K.," Bond said hoarsely. "Now we push it."

"Like hell!" It was A Man Called Peter. "Look, baby, I came up here to go-go, yea-yea-yea, wail, swing, rock. Ain't nothin' in this Local 802 union book says I gotta do donkey work."

"I'll shove that book down—" Bond made a move toward him.

"Cool it, daddy. You're looking at a scab."

Shots skimmed over their heads. "Rifles," said Bond. "They must be planning to come up now. Doc, give me back the field glasses."

He adjusted the zoom-in lens. Camp Camp, he saw, was gone! Smothered by the hellish hordes of insects. Their first phalanx was now moving on Spector, Dr. Nu and the Vi Teh Minh men, Russkis and Fidelistas. Dr. Nu bowed formally, bent down to speak to the leaders of the various species.

He saw the Oriental's mouth agape. My God, the man must be screaming his head off. They're on him! The yellow is disappearing. He's turning black... with insects! Now there's just a blob writhing on the ground. *Sayonara*, Dr. Watts Nu! You and

SPECTOR wanted the world to crawl... and now the crawlers have had their revenge.

Spector! Where was he? He's left his Oriental genius to be gnawed to the bone. He's fleeing down the mountain. You know damn well what's on his mind, Bond. The helicopter! A quick flight to EET with all the swag he's stashed away in the temple and he's back in business with a newer and more dangerous Society for Promulgating Every Conceivable Type Of Rottenness. You can't let that happen, Bond.

"Heave to, everybody! Push, push, push; let's get the ball rolling!"

Sweat rolled from muscles pushed to the bursting point. Men and women grunted, swore, prayed... in vain. Nothing happened.

The hell with it, thought Bond. Smashed, lacerated shoulders or no I'm throwing them to the wheel. He backed off, shouted, "Get out of the way!" and broke into a trot, revved up into a sprint, his head and shoulders hunched up a la a blocking back about to cut down a safety man. And he rammed into the stupendous yellow thing.

Ten tons of matzohball shuddered, rolled over the lip of the precipice!

Down, down, down plummeted the yellow avenger, bouncing from ledge to ledge, gaining incredible speed. It crushed hundreds of thousands of insects with a single bound; then bounced up, up, up in the sky; then down again into the panicking soldiers, strewing them about like tenpins, and down, down, down into the airstrip.

Bond's glasses picked up Nochum Spector, a briefcase in his hand, looking up in horror. Then Spector fell to his knees and began to pray. Too late for that now, you little bastard! The matzohball bounced and came down upon him. Bond saw Nochum and the helicopter disappear under the yellow avalanche. There was a rumble, the sound of magma loosening the bowels of the earth. The matzohball careened into the Temple of Hate. A pillar toppled; then another. The minarets at the roofs corners cracked, fell into the lot. And with a roar the Temple of Hate collapsed into a pile of green debris. Under it were the shattered body and dreams of Nochum Spector, Dr. Nu's IPECAC and the Will Chiller, insatiable Herbie and the Malaysian death vine, plus assorted bigots from every land. Bond, a Raleigh in his lips, had a strange feeling that only Lawrence Talbot got out in time.

"Kinderlach." He grinned shyly at his flock, who fixed worshipful eyes upon him. "You can never be sure about dice, but when you roll a matzohball you've got a natural winner!"

18
It's All Over But The Shooting

Merriment reigned in Our Lady of the Eastern Order... and bravado. Now that the ordeal had rolled away like the matzohball, each one cited his own part in the fantastic, bolt-from-the-blue scheme that had destroyed the archvillains and their Communist cadres.

"If it hadn't been for the good old Rock of Ages Records' caravan, you never woulda had the man power to put together that Jewish yo-yo," boasted O'Marty, deep in his cups.

"How about my participation? If it hadn't been for my artistic touches, O'Marty, you sweet Irish bitch, that ball would not have been so round and firm and fully packed," snipped back Baldroi LeFagel, shallow in *his* cups, a black lace Mansfield bra.

"You should all be ashamed of yourselves," said Sister Sweetcakes. "We should all thank our dear Lord for sending us the Samson who destroyed the temple of the Philistines... Israel Bond."

"Amen," they chorused, and fell silent.

The "Samson" leaned against the wall near the precipice, his eyes still glued upon the holocaust below. The matzohball was beginning to come apart under the torrid midday sun. He thought of Nochum. M. must never know her beloved nephew had been the culprit. He would tell her that Rotten Roger Colfax was a Russian all along and that the traitor business was literally a Red herring to cause doubt and suspicion among the M 33 and 1/3 team. He rehearsed his speech for the tenth time: "You would have been proud of the heroic way he met his Lord in that terrible jungle, Mother."

"Talking to yourself, Mr. Bond?"

"Hello, dear Sister. Come to say good-bye?"

"Yes, Mr. Bond. But let's make that au revoir. I hate good-byes. I know our paths will cross again someday. Now I must go back into the convent and make that long-playing record for Marty. I have asked that the proceeds be set aside for the creation of a Boys' Town on El Tiparillo. Indeed, my brother Baldroi has evinced interest in helping me operate it."

He would, Bond thought.

"Until our paths converge, I want you to have this little token of my esteem and... uh... affection. Please take this, Mr. Bond."

In the palm of his hand was a mirror framed in a lovely coral rectangle. "It is exquisite, as you are, Sister."

"Whenever you look into it, Mr. Bond, you will see my favorite person in all the world." A rose of a blush surfaced on her cheeks. She pressed his hand against her heart. Then she turned and walked slowly back to the convent. She stood at the door, waved and was gone from his sight.

"Adieu, Sister Sweetcakes," he whispered. "May the Bluebird of Happiness bring you Jan Peerce."

He looked into the mirror and saw her (and his) favorite person in all the world. And—someone else! An evil animal whose demented grin bared a golden treasure trove.

Torquemada LaBonza! The "Man With the Golden Gums!" The "Silent One!" No misnomer there. He had not even been aware of the man's approach. Good Lord! LaBonza must have been taught that soundless walk by a Mohican. He glanced at LaBonza's feet. Moccasins. And written in beaded script on each toe, "Property of Uncas."

Israel Bond, you egotistical fool! While you were basking in the plaudits of your admirers back at OLEO, thinking you'd pulled off another successful conclusion, you forgot all about the world's most feared assassin, LaBonza, whose victims die in an insane fit of laughter. Why?

He was to know immediately.

The voice of Torquemada LaBonza came out of that Midas mouth:

"Eh-h-h... what's up, doc? I'll tell you, doc. Your hands, doc. Eh-h-h, that's 'cause I got this silencer against your backbone, doc."

Bond began to laugh and laugh and laugh. It poured out of him like the blood from any of his wounds. LaBonza, angered, spun him around with his left hand and raked Bond's cheek with his gun sight, reopening the old gash.

Still Bond laughed, though the cheek smarted terribly. He could not help it, no matter what.

Torquemada LaBonza's voice was an exact carbon of Bugs Bunny's!

19
Flash
In The Pan

"LaBonza, I can't help it. Nobody could. How in the world did you ever get a voice like that?"

No answer. For a moment Bond thought his query had drawn a Mel Blanc.

Then LaBonza spoke. "I—uh—guess it don't matter now, doc, 'cause I'm gonna kill you anyway and bring that hot-shot mezuzah of yours back to KGB. Pretty humiliatin', ain't it, doc? The Israeli superman is brought down by a cwazy wabbit, eh, doc?"

Though convulsed by simultaneous mirth and fear, Bond nevertheless managed to get the story.

His father was an impressionist, LaBonza pointed out, but made a meager living at it. There were many Cagney-Robinson-Cooper-Grant imitators working the cheap theatre circuit and the father was ruefully aware he had blown his talent on a surfeited market. However, LaBonza added, his father adored the cartoon characters in those delightful shorts one saw accompanying every movie in the '30's and '40's. No one was specializing in these imitations and so, almost from birth, he took Torquemada to the movies three times a week, hoping to leave the boy with a profitable legacy.

"You can't envision what it was like for me in those formative years with a tyrant for a father. Ah, phooey!" (He was Donald Duck, now, quacking irately at his rotten lot in life.) "And, thufferin' thuccotash, thir (now he was an equally incensed Daffy Duck), from the very beginning every time I'd try to thpeak normally, that thtupid father of mine would dig his thumbth into my cheekth until my mouth ached. Thoon I wath afraid to even try thpeaking like a normal perthon. And e-e-e-e-ven wh-wh-wh-en he d-d-d-died (Porky Pig had taken over the narrative at this point) I was so used to speaking like this, mousketeers (Porky passed the ball to Mickey), that I continued on this way. I was ashamed to tell people I couldn't speak like they could and afraid they'd laugh at me when I spoke the only way I could. Kinda awful, huh, Pluto?"

"Why did you become an assassin, LaBonza?" No harm showing a little sympathy to this strangest of human beings.

"Oooh, I thawt I taw a puttycat." (It was Tweety Bird's turn.) "Why? 'Tause I hated my daddy 'tause he made my wife weal miserable. I wanted wevenge on a wotten world. I wanted to—hah! hah!—kill wots of wittle gway wabbits—I hate wittle gway wabbits —and kill even more people." (Elmer Fudd muscled in.) "But, son, why are yuh—ah say, why are yuh askin' me all these dadburned fool questions? You-all ain't tryin' ter put somethin' over on old Torquemada, is yuh? Ah say, is yuh?" (Leghorn had picked up the ball.)

"Certainly not, LaBonza. It's just that your story is so fantastic I want to hear all of it. Why the golden teeth and gums?"

"Jiminy Cricket! (Bond had no trouble identifying this one) I'm your conscience, Torquemada, so I'll answer the gentleman's question. It's 'cause your father squeezed your cheeks so often your teeth softened and fell out. And, honest, Pinoke, so did your gums. So when you killed your first man you had the whole business done in gold so's you'd be sumpin' special, huh? Watch out, Pinoke, the Blue Fairy's back!"

"Well, LaBonza, whoever put in that golden mouth of yours cheated you, buddy boy."

"Ah, *mon ami,* if you are making ze fun of Pepé Le Pew, I keel you *très* slow and easy, a bullet in ze leg, ze hand, ze rib, ze elbow, ze ankle."

Bond smiled nonchalantly. "Why should I make fun? I'm a damn serious guy when I face death, LaBonza. Now, look for yourself. Here's a mirror. If you look very closely you'll see you got the cheapest kind of gold. Maybe it isn't even gold. Maybe it's pyrite—fool's gold. See for yourself."

LaBonza grabbed the mirror. He turned it around and held it toward him, opening his mouth wide.

Bond tensed. If he had figured it out right he had one last chance.

As LaBonza's mouth opened wide the sun flashed against the generous golden expanse, the flash ricocheting off the mirror into LaBonza's eyes. He was blinded for one significant second.

Bond hit him low and hard, the impact with the man's knees sending pangs through his sore shoulders. LaBonza was hurled back, back... and over the wall. His hands clawed for a grip on a root, lost it and he fell into space. Bond heard screaming oinks, quacks, tweets, adieus... then heard them no more as the black dot bounced off a ledge and plunged to the bottom of Mount Maidenhead.

"Adieu, yourself, Torquemada LaBonza," whispered Israel Bond to the valley below. "You could have made the big 'hit' of your career if you'd finished me off. But you gummed it up!"

And now it really *is* over, he knew. This odyssey that started on warm friendly beaches, *segued* to the chill of a Moscow night and climaxed on a jungle mountain top.

Yet, he pondered, could any of it have been real? It had been an adventure peopled by a conglomeration of characters only to be found in the marred convolutions of a psychotic writer's mind.[*] Had any of these menaces been more than cartoons? Any of them? Svetlova with the gash of a mouth, Dr. Nu, Herbie, IPECAC, Spector, Topjob and, finally, LaBonza, a true product of Disney, Lantz, Terry?

How could he put a fitting finis on this nightmare in keeping with its cartoonish genre?

His gray eyes gleamed, the smile forming as he knew what he *must* say. Somewhere in heaven Zvi Gates, all atremble, waited. Israel Bond said: "Th-th-th-that's all, f-f-folks!"

---

[*]   Look, booby. Don't get so damn personal with the Freudian analysis. You like that imbalanced author well enough when he's shoving hot broads into your bed like hotcakes. You could very well be replaced by a Taureg private eye.—S. W.

About the Author

We asked Sol Weinstein, author of the Hebrew Secret Agent Israel Bond (Oy Oy Seven) thrillers to describe his fulsome career in three sentences. They are: 1 1/2 – 3 months for kiting checks ... 2 1/2 months for illegally checking kites at a Tokyo kids' fair ... and 1 week for pushing Stepan Novotny, infamous forger, from the top of the Prague National Bank. (The Czech bounced.)

In addition to Oy Oy Seven's capers in *Loxfinger*, *Matzohball, On the Secret Service of His Majesty the Queen,* and *You Only Live Until You Die*, he wrote a highly sentimental set of music and lyrics to "The Curtain Falls", sung by Kevin Spacey in the biopic *Beyond the Sea* in his role as Bobby Darin.

Sol currently resides in New Zealand, is a member of Temple Sinai in Wellington, and pronounces a favourite ethnic food as "kiegel", not "kugel".

If you enjoyed this book...

...or if you enjoy getting books that you don't enjoy, then look for the full run of Israel Bond Oy-Oy-7 books wherever you got this book. (Unless you found it on a bus or something, because, really, what are the odds of repeating that sort of stroke of amazingly good luck?)

Also available for the Kindle, the Nook, the iPad, and other electronic devices.

Oy-Oy-7.com

www.ingramcontent.com/pod-product-compliance
Lightning Source LLC
Chambersburg PA
CBHW031556040426
42452CB00006B/319